C.E. GRAYSON JR.

Lead Like You Got A Pair

Change Culture. Save Lives.

First published by KDP 2025

Copyright © 2025 by C.E. Grayson Jr.

All rights reserved. No part of this publication may be reproduced, stored or transmitted in any form or by any means, electronic, mechanical, photocopying, recording, scanning, or otherwise without written permission from the publisher. It is illegal to copy this book, post it to a website, or distribute it by any other means without permission.

C.E. Grayson Jr. asserts the moral right to be identified as the author of this work.

Designations used by companies to distinguish their products are often claimed as trademarks. All brand names and product names used in this book and on its cover are trade names, service marks, trademarks and registered trademarks of their respective owners. The publishers and the book are not associated with any product or vendor mentioned in this book. None of the companies referenced within the book have endorsed the book.

First edition

ISBN: 9798273528239

This book was professionally typeset on Reedsy. Find out more at reedsy.com

Contents

Dedication	iv
Author's Note	v
About the AF Leadership Series	vi
Series Overview	vii
Message to the Reader	viii
Acknowledgments	ix
Chapter 1: Integrity Is Doing It Right When No One's...	1
Chapter 2: The Courage to Have the Hard Conversations	10
Chapter 3: Accountability Without Excuses	20
Chapter 4: Consistency Builds Culture	30
Chapter 5: Communication Is Leadership's Superpower	39
Chapter 6: Recognition, Gratitude, and the Power of...	48
Chapter 7: The Standard You Walk Past Is the Standard You...	56
Chapter 8: Leading Through Adversity	63
Chapter 9: From Compliance to Commitment	70
Chapter 10: Empowering Others to Lead	78
Chapter 11: The Courage to Correct	88
Chapter 12: Stay Above the Line	95
Chapter 13: The Power of Humility	108
Chapter 14: The Servant Leader	114
Chapter 15: The Leader's Legacy	120
Closing Quote	126
Thank You for Reading	127
Metadata & Publishing Info	128
AF Leadership Series Catalog	129

Dedication

For every foreman, roofer, leader, and worker who ever decided to do the right thing—even when no one was watching.

Author's Note

This book wasn't written from theory or textbooks—it was built from the ground up, on rooftops, in rain, heat, and real-world experience.

It's for the people who show up every day, who take pride in their craft, and who care enough to do things the right way even when nobody's watching.

Lead strong. Change culture. Save lives.

— C.E. Grayson Jr.

About the AF Leadership Series

The AF Leadership Series was built from the ground up — not in boardrooms or classrooms, but in the field.

These pages come from real life — the rooftops, the job sites, and the tough lessons learned when nobody was watching.

This series isn't about buzzwords or safety posters. It's about what happens when leadership grows a spine — when people stop talking about culture and start living it.

Each book dives into a different side of the fight to lead right: mindset, accountability, communication, integrity, and pride. Together, they form a no-BS roadmap for anyone who wants to stop managing and start leading — the kind of leadership that actually saves lives, builds trust, and changes everything.

Because when you lead like you give a damn, people notice. When you lead like you've got a pair, people follow.

Series Overview

Book 1 – AF Mindset: The foundation — Go all-in. Own your attitude, your choices, and your results. No excuses.

Book 2 – You're Boring AF, Gary!: Communication & energy —
Stop putting people to sleep. Leadership should light a fire, not kill the spark.

Book 3 – Lead Like You Got a Pair: Courage & accountability — Leadership isn't about rank — it's about having the guts to set the standard.

Book 4 – Safe AF: The everyday guide — For every safety professional thrown into the deep end — here's how to swim like a pro.

Message to the Reader

You don't need permission to lead. You don't need a title, a fancy degree, or a gold star.

What you need is grit — the kind that shows up early, owns mistakes, and keeps the standard high even when no one's watching.

This book isn't a checklist. It's a challenge.

It's about stepping up, standing firm, and remembering that real leadership doesn't come from authority — it comes from integrity.

If you're here to make excuses, this book isn't for you. If you're here to make a difference, welcome to the movement.

— C.E. Grayson Jr.

Acknowledgments

There's no such thing as a self-made leader. Every good lesson I've learned came from somebody who showed up before me — or believed in me when I didn't deserve it yet.

To Heather Noelle Hincks, my rock, my partner, and my reason — thank you for believing in me through every late night, every rewrite, and every crazy idea I turned into a mission.

To Maeli Jade, my daughter — your light, your laughter, and your heart remind me every day what kind of legacy I want to leave behind.

To the men and women in the field crews, foremen, and roofers who grind through the elements and make it happen — you are the real heartbeat of this series. This is for you.

To the people who told me 'you can't' — thanks for the motivation.

And finally, to every leader who's ever had the guts to care — keep going. You're the reason this book exists.

Chapter 1: Integrity Is Doing It Right When No One's Watching

"Integrity isn't about who sees you do the right thing—it's about who you become when nobody does."

Integrity is the first language of leadership. Every policy, every rule, every safety talk eventually funnels down to one choice: do you do it right when no one's around? In our world, integrity isn't a buzzword. It's a behavioral constant. It's the invisible backbone that keeps roofs upright and people alive.

A poster might define integrity as "doing the right thing." On paper, that looks simple enough. But out on a roof—when the rain's coming sideways, the wind's in your ears, and the client's pacing below—it isn't theory anymore. It's a test. Integrity doesn't live in slogans; it lives in the muscle memory of people who have learned that shortcuts cost more than time.

When I talk about integrity, I'm not talking about perfection. I'm talking about predictability. The kind that tells your team they can count on you to do the same thing right every single time, even if nobody's watching.

Integrity looks like the foreman who ties off at an awkward anchor point instead of saying "close enough." It looks like the roofer who stops to resecure a ladder because it "doesn't look right." It's the worker who calls for a time-out when something feels off even though production is screaming for speed. These are the quiet, inconvenient moments that define a culture.

Most people mistake integrity for image. They think it's about how good they look doing the right thing. But real integrity is quiet. It doesn't need an audience. You'll rarely see it celebrated because, by its nature, it happens when nobody's there to clap.

The best crews I've seen operate on one shared currency: trust. Trust is what lets you walk under another person's ladder without looking up. It's knowing that the person in front of you checked the footing, the tie-off, the harness. And trust doesn't appear out of nowhere—it's built, slowly and deliberately, through consistent integrity. Every time you hold the line, you deposit a little bit of trust into that invisible account. Every time you let something slide, you make a withdrawal. Eventually, that balance decides how safe your people feel.

Integrity and trust are twins. When one fails, the other collapses. You can talk about safety until you lose your voice, but if you allow one shortcut "just this once," you've told everyone that your standards are negotiable. The next shortcut will come faster, the excuses will get easier, and the line you were protecting disappears.

On the flip side, when you do it right every time—when you prove by repetition that the rule is the rule, not a suggestion—your people learn to breathe easier. They stop worrying about which version of you is going to show up today. That stability is what turns rules into culture.

Integrity isn't glamorous. It's repetitive. It's the same conversation about ladder angles, the same insistence on documentation, the same reminder that "almost safe" isn't safe. But that's exactly why it matters: because culture isn't built in moments of inspiration; it's built in daily decisions nobody writes down.

The hardest thing about integrity is how lonely it feels. It's the decision you make when the rest of the crew is already heading down for lunch. It's re-tying your harness when nobody told you to. It's throwing away a worn rope instead of "getting one more job out of it." No one applauds, but those micro-decisions keep people alive.

Doing the right thing costs something. It costs time, comfort, and sometimes popularity. People will call you rigid, slow, "by-the-book." Let

CHAPTER 1: INTEGRITY IS DOING IT RIGHT WHEN NO ONE'S...

them. Because those same voices will look to you when something goes wrong. Leadership built on comfort falls apart under pressure; leadership built on integrity stands like rebar in concrete—it keeps everything else from crumbling.

Picture this. You're behind schedule. Homeowner's impatient. Storm's coming. You've got a choice: skip resetting an anchor because "it's only a few steps," or stop and fix it. The easy route saves five minutes. The right route might save a life. That's integrity in motion.

Integrity isn't something you switch off when you clock out. Who you are on-site is who you are off-site. The habits follow you. If you lie about a measurement, you'll lie on a timesheet. If you overlook a hazard, you'll overlook a promise. Integrity is an identity, not a costume.

There's a story I tell during training. It's about a man named Rick who set his ladder ten degrees too flat. It looked fine until he leaned right. The ladder slipped, and he learned more in two seconds than most people learn in a year. He walked away lucky, but luck isn't integrity—it's mercy. What mattered was what happened next. The foreman stopped the job, made every worker reset every ladder until they could feel the correct angle instinctively. People grumbled, but by the end of the day they had learned something that stuck. That's what integrity looks like: turning a mistake into muscle memory for an entire crew.

Integrity isn't performance. Visibility doesn't equal virtue. Plenty of people look solid when management's on the roof, but the test comes when the truck pulls away. You can't fake integrity under pressure. When the wind kicks up and the roof slicks over, performance ends and standards show.

Each time you follow through, you build credibility. Each time you look away, you lose it. Most leaders think they have more trust than they actually do—until the day they need it. You can build credibility in teaspoons and lose it in buckets.

Integrity hurts because it holds a mirror. It demands that you do the right thing even when it costs you popularity. The temptation to justify is constant. *It's only a second. I'll fix it later. Nobody's fallen yet.* Those sentences are how integrity erodes. Each one lowers your ceiling until you can't stand up straight anymore. Integrity says, "I hear the excuse, and I'm doing it right anyway."

Integrity starts in thought before it shows in action. The little lies you tell yourself—*I'll double-check later*—are the first cracks in the structure. Catch them early, and you've already won half the battle.

When one person chooses integrity, the impact ripples. Someone else sees it, copies it, passes it on. You might never know who's watching you tie off, clean a walkway, or admit a mistake—but they are. That's how cultures shift: through quiet imitation.

Respect isn't something you demand; it's something you earn by example. Yelling creates compliance, not commitment. But integrity—doing what's right when it's hard—creates respect automatically. At first, people grumble. Later, they defend the standard for you. That's when leadership starts multiplying.

Leadership AF Lesson:
Integrity doesn't need an audience. It builds its own reputation—one action at a time.

Teaching integrity takes intention. You can't expect people to "just get it." Demonstrate before you dictate. Explain the *why* behind each rule. Every standard has a story; tell it. Let others repeat it in their own words. Reward the right behaviors. Correct fast and calm. Integrity spreads the same way shortcuts do—through repetition. Choose which one multiplies.

Integrity is the DNA of leadership. Without it, accountability turns into punishment and communication turns into spin. With it, those same tools become fuel for trust.

There's peace in integrity. When you know you've done it right, there's no anxiety about being caught, no stress about what people will say. Predictability replaces pressure. People stop guessing whether you'll back them up—they already know.

At the end of every day, integrity asks for a moment of reflection. Walk the site. Are ladders tied, anchors tagged, harnesses clipped? Then look inward:

CHAPTER 1: INTEGRITY IS DOING IT RIGHT WHEN NO ONE'S...

did you lead today the way you want your crew to work tomorrow? If yes, go home proud. If not yet, make it tomorrow's first mission.

The farther you go in leadership, the more integrity costs—and the more it pays. In the beginning, doing it right feels like compliance. Later, it becomes conviction. That's the turning point where a person stops working for a paycheck and starts working for pride.

A roofer once told me, "I can't see the boss from up here." I told him, "That's when the boss gets to see who you really are." Integrity isn't for show; it's for your reflection. It's the standard you carry when there's nobody left to impress.

In safety work, integrity doesn't announce itself with speeches; it proves itself in patterns. You don't build a culture of safety by handing out checklists—you build it by repeating right actions until they become instinct. Every time someone clips in automatically, every time a ladder gets tied off without prompting, every time paperwork is filled in because it *should be*, not because someone's watching—that's integrity teaching itself.

You can tell when a crew has reached that point. The rhythm is quiet. There's less yelling. People move with intention. A new hire shows up and, without being told, starts doing things the right way because everyone else already is. That's when you know integrity has become part of the air they breathe.

Still, no culture is permanent. The moment you stop feeding it, complacency sneaks back in. That's why reflection matters. The best leaders I've known end every shift by asking themselves the same three questions:

Did I keep every promise I made today?

Did I correct what needed correcting—or walk past it?

Did I model what I expect from others?

Those aren't ceremonial questions; they're maintenance checks for your own leadership engine. Skip them too long and things start rattling loose.

There's a daily practice I teach—something I call the two-minute integrity huddle. It happens right after roll call. Two minutes, no more. You stand in front of the crew and lay it out: "Here's the plan. Here's where we can get hurt. Here's how we prevent it. Everyone here has stop-work authority—use it. If you see it, you own it. Tie off, check, verify, and finish like pros." You do that every morning, and eventually your team believes that integrity isn't optional—it's the expectation.

The truth is, living with integrity can feel invisible. You'll spend years doing the right thing and wonder if anyone notices. They do—they just won't say it until the moment you're under pressure. Then, when everything's on the line, they'll trust you because you've been steady for so long that it's unthinkable you'd fail them now. That's the invisible dividend of consistency.

Integrity pays in loyalty. When your people know you won't sell them out for a deadline, they'll go the extra mile for you. They'll train new hires, guard your standards, and take ownership because you've given them something real to believe in. That's how legacies form: through a thousand quiet decisions that nobody saw but everyone felt.

A lot of leaders make the mistake of separating integrity from communication. They think "doing right" is enough. It isn't. You have to explain *why* it's right. People rarely resist safety because they're lazy—they resist because they don't understand the reason behind the rule. When you take the time to connect the action to the consequence—when you say, "We tie off here because a man once fell in the same situation"—you turn compliance into conviction. Integrity without explanation is just obedience; integrity with understanding becomes culture.

One of my favorite stories comes from a crew that built a guardrail out of scrap two-by-fours and rope. It looked solid until someone leaned on it. The rail snapped, the worker fell back, bruised but alive. Everyone said afterward, "It looked fine." The problem wasn't laziness—it was assumption. Nobody tested it, nobody verified. The foreman changed the rule that day: no assumption goes unverified. That's integrity institutionalized. It's how you transform pain into prevention.

There's also a peace that comes from being a leader who does the right thing in silence. Once you've built the habit, you stop worrying about being caught because there's nothing to hide. You become predictable in the best possible

way. People stop guessing whether you'll back them up; they know you will. Your consistency becomes their confidence. That predictability—steady tone, steady standard—is what creates psychological safety. And that's what every team needs before it can perform at its best.

Integrity isn't something you can delegate. You can't "assign" honesty or "outsource" responsibility. You model it, you protect it, and you teach it. The surest way to keep integrity alive in your crew is to teach it deliberately and repetitively. That means you show it, explain it, ask them to repeat it, reward it, and correct it fast. Integrity is like concrete—it sets best when it's poured continuously. Stop the pour, and cracks form.

When you make a correction, keep it calm and brief. Integrity doesn't need volume; it needs clarity. A quiet correction in the moment teaches more than an angry lecture after the fact. People remember tone longer than words. If you stay steady, they'll hear the message instead of the noise.

Never forget that integrity spreads the same way shortcuts do—by imitation. Every decision you make is an example someone else will repeat. Choose carefully which behaviors you're multiplying.

If you think about it, integrity sits at the root of every other leadership skill. Accountability, communication, consistency—all of them rely on it. Without integrity, accountability becomes punishment, communication becomes manipulation, and consistency becomes rigidity. But with integrity, those same elements turn into the architecture of trust.

Leadership AF Lesson:
Integrity is the DNA of leadership. Remove it, and everything else mutates.

Integrity is also humility. It's the ability to admit when you missed something and to correct it without ego. The moment a leader starts believing they're above correction, culture starts to decay. The strongest leaders are the most transparent ones—the ones who say, "That one's on me. Here's how we fix it." The crew doesn't lose respect for a leader who admits fault; they lose respect for one who hides it.

Let's talk about integrity under pressure. Deadlines, weather, production goals—all of them expose who you really are. Anyone can quote a policy when things are calm. The real test comes when you're staring down a schedule and the temptation to "just get it done" creeps in. Pressure doesn't create character; it reveals it. If you can slow down, breathe, and make the hard call even when it costs time, you're teaching your people that standards don't melt under heat.

One of my favorite field maxims is this: *the standard you walk past is the standard you set.* Every time you ignore a missed tie-off or a sloppy ladder, you've silently approved it. You can preach safety all day, but the real sermon happens when you decide what to tolerate. Integrity demands that your actions match your words. It's slower, harder, and sometimes lonely—but it's how you build a reputation that outlasts the job.

There's a story about a foreman who shut down a downtown project because of incoming storms. The general contractor was furious. The crew wanted to keep working. He said no. They secured everything, tarped the deck, and went home. The next day, seventy-mile-an-hour winds hit. Had they stayed, someone would have gone off that roof. On Monday, nobody argued with his calls anymore. That's integrity translating into authority. You can't buy that kind of respect—you earn it by making the right decision when it's hardest to make.

The longer you lead, the more you realize that integrity is maintenance work. It's like checking your harness—something you do even when you already know it's fine, because the habit matters more than the result. Reflection, repetition, and correction keep it strong. Skip any one of those, and the whole system weakens.

Every good leader I've met has some version of a personal mirror test. Before they leave for the day, they ask, "Did I lead with integrity today?" They don't always like the answer, but the act of asking keeps them honest. Leadership isn't about perfection; it's about direction. The question keeps you pointed north.

There's a final thought I leave with every crew: integrity isn't about grand gestures. It's about the quiet choice to do what's right—again, and again, and again—until doing wrong feels unnatural. The repetition of right behavior builds muscle memory for ethics. And that muscle memory is what saves lives.

Integrity doesn't ask for perfection, only persistence. Every day you show up, every task you complete with honesty, every rule you uphold without being told, you're adding another brick to the foundation of a culture that lasts. One day someone else will walk that same roofline and feel safer because of decisions you made years before. They won't know your name. They won't need to. They'll just work confidently, quietly, safely—and that's the proof that you led well.

That's integrity. Not the noise of being seen, but the peace of being certain.

Chapter 2: The Courage to Have the Hard Conversations

"If you're too afraid to speak the truth, you're too weak to lead."

Leadership is equal parts silence and sound. The challenge isn't choosing which tool to use—it's knowing when silence turns from discipline into avoidance. Every leader carries two invisible tool belts: one full of actions and one full of words. Most of us learn early how to swing a hammer or check a harness, but we're slower to learn how dangerous it is to leave that second belt untouched.

Silence feels safe. You tell yourself, *I'll bring it up later*, or *It's not that big of a deal*. What you're really doing is renting quiet time on credit. The interest will come due in the form of resentment, confusion, or an accident. Avoiding confrontation might protect your comfort, but it never protects your people.

Every organization that collapses under cultural weight has one common thread: the leaders stopped talking about what mattered. The small behaviors—the half-clipped harness, the untied ladder, the *"it'll be fine"* attitude—are warning lights. Courageous conversations are the release valves that keep pressure from blowing the system apart. They're uncomfortable, inconvenient, and absolutely essential.

Nobody enjoys confrontation. Even the toughest foremen feel that pulse jump when they have to tell someone they're wrong. Your throat tightens, your brain starts writing excuses: *He already knows. I'll mention it next time. It's not worth the drama.* But it is. The moment you decide to keep quiet, you've just taught everyone that standards are negotiable. That's how cultures drift— from excellence to average—one unsaid sentence at a time.

Fear drives avoidance. Fear of conflict, fear of rejection, fear of saying it wrong. But fear and leadership can't share the same harness. Every time you speak truth calmly, you prove that your mission outweighs your comfort. The crew learns from that. They watch you choose professionalism over popularity.

True courage isn't loud—it's deliberate. It's the quiet decision to face a problem before it festers. It's saying the thing that needs saying when your voice would rather hide. Leaders who master that balance of calm and candor create cultures that don't need constant policing. They create teams that self-correct.

I once saw a crew that looked perfect on paper—fast, efficient, early finishes every week. Beneath the numbers, though, shortcuts were stacking up. Tieoffs skipped "just for flashing," ladders left loose "because we're moving it in a minute." Everyone knew. Nobody said a word. The foreman didn't want to "start something." Then one windy Tuesday, a helper slid off the edge. He caught the gutter and lived, but the silence died that day. When the foreman finally admitted he'd seen the bad habits for weeks, his authority vanished. The crew no longer trusted him because he had chosen comfort over courage.

That's the true cost of silence. You might think you're keeping peace, but you're really trading safety for popularity. Respect without honesty is counterfeit. The most respectful thing a leader can do is tell the truth—kindly, clearly, consistently. Telling someone the truth says, *I care enough about you to risk being uncomfortable.*

You can do it without hostility. You can say, *"You've been getting sloppy lately; I know you're better than that."* Or, *"You're setting a bad example right now; fix it before someone gets hurt."* Those words sting for a moment, but they protect for a lifetime. Every leader must choose between the discomfort of one honest minute or the regret of a lifetime spent wishing they'd spoken up.

Every unsaid truth becomes a weight you carry. It leaks into every decision, every meeting, until you're managing ghosts instead of people. Avoidance is mold—it spreads quietly until it weakens the whole structure. Eventually, the team stops taking you seriously because they've learned you don't enforce the line you talk about.

The goal isn't to attack; it's to align. Hard conversations aren't random explosions of frustration—they're deliberate acts of maintenance. The same precision you use setting a ladder applies to confrontation: footing matters, angle matters, balance matters. When you're deliberate, accountability stops feeling like punishment and starts feeling like teamwork.

Here's a framework I teach every new supervisor: **CALM**—Context, Action, Loss, Move Forward. It keeps conversations professional and factual.

Context means describe what you saw, where, and when. "Yesterday, while we were staging materials on the east side…" **Action** means name the behavior, not the person. "…you climbed the ladder without tying off." **Loss** means explain the risk.

"If you slip, you're heading fifteen feet down to concrete. That's a hospital ride."

Move Forward means finish with a positive step.

"Let's reset your anchor and review tie-off before we continue."

Four short sentences. No drama, no insults, no monologues. Just leadership. When you stay CALM, you replace accusation with collaboration. People stop bracing for punishment and start listening for solutions.

I saw a foreman use this once in the middle of a steep-slope tear-off. A veteran roofer had unhooked to "save time." The foreman could've shouted; instead, he walked over and said, "I saw you unhook on that west pitch. If that line slips, you're gone. Re-hook and walk me through what slowed you down." The worker explained that the anchor layout was awkward. Together they adjusted it and finished the day tied in. The whole crew learned two lessons: the standard isn't optional, and correction doesn't have to mean humiliation. That's leadership under pressure—calm, factual, effective.

Timing matters as much as tone. If you call someone out in front of a crowd, you'll get defense, not growth. Correct as soon as possible while the moment's fresh, but do it privately unless others are at risk. Then end on a positive note. Let them leave knowing how to win next time. Accountability

CHAPTER 2: THE COURAGE TO HAVE THE HARD CONVERSATIONS

without dignity becomes resentment.

Tone is your other tool. Your voice should sound steady, not sarcastic. If you can't stay calm, wait until you can. Nobody learns from a lecture shouted over wind and compressors. Emotional control is a safety skill too.

That kind of restraint doesn't come naturally—it's practiced. Leaders who take time to breathe before reacting model composure for the whole team. It's the pause that separates reaction from response. One deep breath can save a relationship, a reputation, and sometimes a life.

The long game is building a culture where honesty feels safe. You want crews who talk straight to each other instead of about each other. That starts with you. When leaders admit their own mistakes openly—"I missed that detail on the schedule, that's on me"—they teach everyone that honesty won't get you punished. That visible humility builds psychological safety faster than any policy.

Create open-door moments by asking, "What needs fixing?" and meaning it. When someone speaks up, thank them before you correct them. Gratitude first, instruction second—that order matters.

The difference between coaching and confronting is simple: confronting wants to win; coaching wants to help. When your motive is to dominate, you lose the relationship. When your motive is to develop, you both get stronger. Coaching sounds like, "You've been solid for months, but your focus is slipping. Let's figure out what's going on." Confronting sounds like, "You're screwing up again." One opens a door; the other slams it.

Remember: you can't coach what you haven't earned the right to correct.

That right comes from trust, and trust grows from consistency.

If the only time people hear from you is when something's wrong, you've already lost influence. Keep a balance between correction and recognition. Catch people doing things right. Praise the behavior you want multiplied. *"Good tie-off—that's how it's done,"* said publicly once, can prevent a dozen violations later.

I teach every new leader the 24-hour rule: if behavior needs addressing, do it within a day. After that, your credibility fades. If it were truly important, why'd you wait? But don't strike while you're angry either. Review the facts, cool down, and come back ready to fix, not to vent. The rule keeps accountability alive and relevant.

Common pitfalls trap many supervisors. They lecture instead of listen. They confuse correction with control. They correct in front of everyone. They make it personal. They fail to follow up. Each of these drains credibility. Accountability without follow-through feels like punishment. Checking back later—"How's that process working now?"—shows you care about growth, not blame.

Every leader eventually faces the rookie mistake: the moment you're tempted to let something slide because "he's new, he'll learn." He will—but either from you or from gravity. A supervisor once caught a new hire tying into a ridge mid-span with too much distance between anchors. Looked fine until you measured it. The foreman almost walked away, then caught himself. "If I ignore it, I'm teaching him it's okay." He walked over, kept it calm: "You tied off here—it's too far apart. Let's fix it together." No yelling, no lecture. That rookie still talks about that day years later. That's the ripple effect of courage.

Leadership isn't the absence of emotion; it's mastery over it. Anger, fear, frustration—they're all normal. The key is not letting them run the meeting. Take one deep breath before every tough talk. That pause separates reaction from response. One breath can save a career.

Courage is a muscle. You don't build it by reading about it; you build it by using it. Role-play conversations with your leads. It might feel awkward, but it's the fastest way to get comfortable being uncomfortable. Practice CALM until it becomes second nature. The more you rehearse in safe moments, the steadier you'll be in real ones.

Courageous communication isn't a single act; it's a rhythm that defines your leadership heartbeat. You won't always get it perfect, but you can't let that stop you from trying. When you speak with clarity and respect, even imperfect words carry truth. Silence, on the other hand, is always perfect for misunderstanding.

You can measure a leader's courage by the speed with which they face problems. Fast, honest conversations prevent slow, painful disasters. Problems are like leaks in a roof—ignore them, and one day you'll find the ceiling caved in. Address them early, and the repair costs nothing but a conversation.

Leadership AF Lesson:
Courage isn't volume. It's velocity—the willingness to act while the window's still open. Speak sooner. Speak calmer. Speak truth with purpose, and you'll never have to shout it later.

Not every conversation has to be disciplinary. Some of the hardest ones are supportive. You'll see it in a worker whose energy fades, whose attention slips. Maybe they're dealing with something at home, or they've lost confidence. It takes courage to ask, "Are you okay?" Leadership is more than pointing out mistakes—it's noticing the human being behind them. Sometimes the bravest thing you can say is, "I've seen you off your game lately, and I care about what's going on." You can't fix everything, but your willingness to ask proves that leadership still includes humanity.

The flip side of courage is listening. If you only speak, you're not having a conversation—you're issuing orders. Listening with the intent to understand, not just to reply, is how you turn information into insight. Workers on the front line often see risks long before management does. If they trust that speaking up won't bring retaliation, they'll tell you. If not, you'll find out from the accident report.

To encourage openness, respond to reports with curiosity, not criticism. "Thanks for catching that. What do you think caused it?" turns a complaint into a collaboration. That tone builds confidence faster than any incentive program.

A crew that can talk freely about risk becomes self-correcting. They hold each other accountable because they've seen their leaders do it without fear. That's when culture starts running on its own momentum—when courage stops being top-down and becomes everyone's reflex.

Still, leadership will always include friction. Sometimes your words land wrong. Sometimes a correction bruises pride. That's not failure—it's feedback. How you handle the next moment determines whether that bruise heals or festers. The worst thing you can do is hide from it.

You'll face moments where you must rebuild trust after a hard talk goes sideways. Maybe your tone was off, or the timing was wrong. Don't bury it under silence. Revisit the person privately. "I came in hot earlier. My intent was right, but my delivery wasn't. Let's reset." That single act of humility re-opens the bridge you accidentally burned. Integrity and courage often walk the same road: both demand you admit when you misstep.

That kind of vulnerability is leadership maturity. Weak leaders double down to protect their ego; strong ones double back to protect the relationship. Every time you circle back with humility, you remind your team that leadership isn't a pedestal—it's a position of service.

Remember this: authority gives you the right to speak, but credibility gives you permission to be heard. Credibility grows when you prove you can deliver hard truths without disrespect. You can be firm and still be kind. You can correct someone and still show them dignity. It isn't weakness to speak gently; it's wisdom. Volume never equals leadership—clarity does.

One of the most respected superintendents I ever met used to say, "Don't raise your voice, raise your standard." His team never mistook calmness for softness because his consistency had already proven his seriousness. When he said, "That's not our way," people fixed it instantly. He didn't need anger—his history spoke louder.

Every difficult talk has three phases: prepare, deliver, and follow up. **Preparation** means reviewing facts, not feelings—what happened, when, and what risk it created. **Delivery** means being direct but steady. **Follow-up** means checking progress and offering help. Most leaders forget that last part. Accountability without follow-up breeds cynicism. When you check back a week later—"How's that working since we talked?"—you turn discipline into development.

There's also a strategic side to courageous communication: documentation. Every serious conversation should leave a short written trail—not as punishment, but as protection. Write what was discussed, what was agreed on, and what the next steps are. Then share it with the person involved so there's mutual understanding. Documentation is proof of fairness. It

CHAPTER 2: THE COURAGE TO HAVE THE HARD CONVERSATIONS

prevents "he-said, she-said" and shows consistency across the organization.

Consistency is another form of courage. You can't correct one person for a behavior you ignore in another. Selective enforcement kills morale faster than any accident. Fairness doesn't mean softness—it means every rule applies to everyone, including you. People respect even harsh policies if they're applied evenly. They rebel against favoritism instantly.

And that's where leadership courage deepens—it's not just about the tough talk on the roof; it's about holding the same standard for yourself behind closed doors. The way you talk about absent crew members, the way you report an error that could be hidden, the way you respond when no one would know the difference—these are all conversations too, just quieter ones, between you and your conscience.

Some of the most courageous conversations you'll ever have are internal. They sound like: *Did I handle that right? Did I choose pride or growth? Did I avoid something because it scared me?* When you can answer those honestly, your leadership starts running on truth instead of pretense.

Leadership AF Lesson:
Courage is consistency under pressure—the ability to hold the same line when it shakes in your hands.

Sometimes, courage means speaking truth *upward*. It's easy to correct a worker; harder to correct your boss. Yet leadership flows both directions. If you see unsafe priorities or unrealistic deadlines, silence makes you complicit. The key is professionalism: facts over feelings. *"We're rushing beyond what's safe, and here's the data."* That's not rebellion—that's responsibility. Good leaders above you will respect it. The bad ones need to hear it anyway.

Upward courage is delicate but vital. It's the difference between loyalty and blind obedience. Loyalty protects people; obedience protects image. When you speak up respectfully, you're not defying authority—you're defending it from preventable harm. Real leaders respect that kind of backbone because it guards the mission, not the ego.

Courage doesn't thrive in chaos—it thrives in clarity. The clearer your expectations are, the easier the hard talks become. Write your standards down. Post them. Teach them. Then reference them during corrections: *"You know the rule. Here's where we missed it."* The rule becomes the referee, not you. That separation removes ego from the exchange and keeps emotion from turning accountability into argument.

Let's not romanticize this. Some conversations will still sting. You'll lose a few people along the way. Not everyone wants to grow. But that's part of leadership—protecting the mission, not the mood. When you hold someone accountable and they choose to leave, you haven't failed; you've refined your culture. Every departure of a person who refuses accountability is a deposit in your culture's strength account.

There's also courage in follow-through. Once you've addressed behavior, don't secretly hope it improves—verify it. Observe, coach, reinforce. Change without reinforcement evaporates. Think of it like patching a roof; you wouldn't leave before checking for leaks. Courage means seeing the fix through to the end.

Hard conversations also demand emotional endurance. One talk rarely changes everything. You'll repeat yourself, remind, retrain, and sometimes rediscipline. That's normal. Progress is measured in reduction, not elimination. If violations drop by half after your intervention, celebrate the movement.

Courage sees improvement, not perfection.

Over time, your steady voice becomes a kind of moral compass for your team. They start anticipating what you'd say even when you're not around. That's when culture takes root. You've built not just compliance but conscience—the ability of your people to self-correct because they understand why standards matter.

Courage grows in reflection, too. After each hard talk, evaluate yourself:
Did I prepare with facts?
Did I stay calm?
Did I end with a clear path forward?
Did I listen?

These questions are your calibration tools. Answer honestly, and each

CHAPTER 2: THE COURAGE TO HAVE THE HARD CONVERSATIONS

conversation will sharpen you for the next one.

Eventually, you'll realize that the courage to confront is also the courage to care. The people who challenge you the hardest are often the ones who respect you most. Because deep down, everyone wants a leader who tells the truth.

Before every safety meeting, I remind supervisors: *"We're not here to be liked. We're here to keep people alive."* If you happen to earn respect along the way, it's because you earned it through consistency and courage, not charm.

At the end of each week, write down one conversation you avoided. Circle it. Ask yourself why. If the reason starts with comfort, you already know what to do Monday morning. Start there. The muscle only grows when you use it.

The truth is, leadership courage doesn't end when the conversation does—it lingers in how you carry yourself afterward. If you walk away resentful, you're still in it. If you walk away clear, you've done your job. Clarity is the quiet after the storm; it's what remains when pride has left the room.

Hard conversations are the backbone of leadership. They protect standards, strengthen relationships, and sustain culture. Avoid them, and everything weakens. Face them, and everything strengthens. The courage to speak is the courage to lead.

The best leaders don't chase comfort—they chase clarity. They know that silence might buy them a day of peace but costs them a culture. They've learned that one clean, honest sentence spoken at the right time can save a life, a career, and a legacy.

That's what separates managers from leaders—the willingness to say what must be said, exactly when it needs saying.

Chapter 3: Accountability Without Excuses

"Accountability is ownership in motion. It's not about blame—it's about backbone."

Accountability is where leadership either grows roots or withers. Every organization preaches it; few live it. Most people hear the word and brace for punishment, because too often accountability gets confused with blame. But real accountability is about ownership—about standing tall in your own decisions, good or bad, and helping others do the same. It's the quiet, daily act of saying, *This one's on me*, and then doing what it takes to make it right.

When you lead people, you carry two responsibilities at once: your own performance and the culture you create. Accountability binds those together. Without it, rules become suggestions, and expectations dissolve into wish lists. You can have the best safety plan, the smartest crew, the most expensive gear—but if accountability doesn't live in the hearts of your people, all you have are props on a weak stage.

Every strong team I've ever worked with shared one common truth: mistakes were addressed quickly and directly. Not emotionally, not politically—factually. Nobody hid. Nobody lied. When something went wrong, the question wasn't *Who do we blame?* It was *How do we fix it, and what do we learn?* That shift—from blame to ownership—changes everything.

The problem is, excuses feel easier in the moment. Human nature loves

CHAPTER 3: ACCOUNTABILITY WITHOUT EXCUSES

self-protection. The brain fires off instinctive justifications: *It wasn't my fault. I didn't have time. The weather changed. Someone else told me.* These small defenses might protect pride, but they poison progress. Every excuse delays growth and teaches everyone watching that responsibility is optional.

Excuses are leadership termites—they don't bite loud, they hollow silently. A single "Yeah, but…" from a supervisor echoes through the crew louder than a dropped hammer. Once people see leaders explain away their own misses, they learn the art of dodging instead of the habit of owning. Culture starts to rot in the spaces where accountability should live.

When you catch yourself or your crew sliding into that mindset, pause. Ask the only question that matters: *What part of this can I control right now?* That question turns victims into problem solvers. Leaders who model it teach their people that accountability isn't something you fear—it's something you practice.

I once worked alongside a supervisor named Dale. His crew respected him because he never ducked ownership. If production fell behind, he'd say, "We misjudged the day. That's on me." Then he'd make a plan, not a speech. No blaming, no finger-pointing—just action. His consistency created freedom: the crew didn't hide mistakes because they knew he wouldn't weaponize them. Accountability replaced fear with honesty. Under his watch, incidents dropped, morale rose, and the culture thickened into trust.

That's the power of accountability done right. It builds a climate where telling the truth feels safer than hiding it. When your people can admit errors without humiliation, you finally start solving the real problems instead of the symptoms.

Accountability also means clarity. You can't hold someone responsible for a standard they don't understand. Expectations must be visible, measurable, and repeated until nobody can claim confusion. Ambiguity is the enemy of accountability. A vague order like "Be careful up there" produces vague results. A clear directive—"Tie off at the ridge anchor every time you cross the valley"—creates accountability you can measure.

Clarity removes excuses before they form. When standards are precise, every choice becomes black-and-white: you either did it or you didn't. That's not harsh—it's fair. People actually prefer clear lines because they make success possible. Accountability thrives where expectations are defined and consistent.

The strongest accountability cultures grow from the top down but also from the inside out. If leadership won't own its mistakes, no one else will. I've seen managers preach safety until an inspection goes wrong, then blame the field for lack of paperwork. The crew notices. Once leaders dodge accountability, credibility collapses. The rule is simple: you can't ask for what you won't model.

I remember one manager—sharp guy, lots of experience—who used to blame "communication breakdowns" every time a report went missing. The truth was, he never followed up. Everyone knew it, but nobody said it out loud. Over time, his crew stopped sending updates because they knew he'd never check them. Accountability decayed by neglect, not defiance. That's the thing about leadership rot—it's quiet at first. Then one day, it smells.

Leaders sometimes fear that owning mistakes will make them look weak. The opposite is true. Accountability builds authority because it shows honesty. When you admit fault openly—"I should have caught that earlier"—you set a tone that honesty outranks ego. People stop wasting energy protecting themselves and start using that energy to fix the issue. That's efficient leadership.

But accountability doesn't mean humiliation. It's not about pinning guilt; it's about prompting growth. A foreman once told me, "I don't scold; I coach." He understood that accountability is direction, not punishment. When someone misses a standard, you guide them back to it. "Here's what happened. Here's what needs to change. Here's how I'll help you." That method builds skill and self-respect simultaneously. Punishment builds resentment; coaching builds competence.

Coaching accountability also means knowing when to correct quietly and when to make a moment visible. Sometimes, a private word preserves dignity. Other times, a public conversation protects others from repeating the same mistake. The art of leadership lies in discerning which moment is which. If your motive is growth, your tone will guide you.

CHAPTER 3: ACCOUNTABILITY WITHOUT EXCUSES

To make accountability real, feedback must be immediate. Waiting weeks to correct a mistake makes the lesson abstract. Address it when it's fresh. Not angrily—factually. "I saw the ladder untied at the east side today. Let's fix it before we move on." Instant correction keeps problems small. Delay turns them into habits.

Consistency matters just as much as timing. Selective accountability kills morale. If one worker gets away with a violation because he's fast or popular, everyone else notices. Fair enforcement earns respect; favoritism breeds rebellion. The rule has to apply to everyone—including you. A leader who enforces rules on others but excuses their own lapses teaches hypocrisy. Integrity and accountability are twin rails; take away one, and the train derails.

There's a phrase I use often: *Inspect what you expect.* It means follow through. Don't just announce standards—verify them. When you check equipment, documentation, and procedures regularly, you send a clear message: these expectations matter. People rise or fall to the level of the attention you give. If you stop inspecting, they assume you've stopped caring.

Accountability is also about data. Track performance metrics: incidents, near misses, inspection results, completion rates. Numbers tell stories words can hide. When trends start slipping, respond before the slide turns into a crash. A leader who uses data as a compass, not a cudgel, helps the team correct course without shame.

Numbers are mirrors—they reflect consistency, not character. What gives them meaning is how you respond. You can use data to prove people wrong, or you can use it to help them grow. The same spreadsheet can divide or develop, depending on whether it's wielded with ego or empathy.

Then there's self-accountability, the hardest of all. It means evaluating your own leadership daily. *Did I enforce every standard I talked about? Did I delay a conversation because it was uncomfortable? Did I recognize good work or just focus on what went wrong?* Honest answers refine your craft more than any seminar ever could.

Self-accountability is leadership's mirror test. You can't fake it for long.

The crew will always see what you avoid. The moment you start justifying your own shortcuts, they'll multiply theirs. But when you take ownership—when you admit, "That one's on me"—you give everyone else permission to do the same.

Leadership AF Lesson:
Accountability isn't a punishment—it's a partnership with reality. When you face the truth faster than your fear, you turn mistakes into material for growth.

The best leaders treat accountability like maintenance, not emergency repair. They schedule it. Weekly safety walks, follow-up notes, small debriefs—tiny doses of truth that keep the system healthy. You don't wait for failure; you prevent it through attention. Routine accountability feels boring, but boredom is the price of consistency.

Emotional control fuels accountability. A leader who explodes every time something goes wrong teaches fear, not responsibility. When you stay calm, you model composure under pressure. Crews mirror the emotional temperature of their supervisor. If you react with focus instead of fury, they'll learn to do the same. Accountability requires self-regulation first.

I once knew a superintendent who had mastered that art. The man was unshakeable. During a roof inspection, a crew had missed anchoring a 40foot ladder—serious mistake. Everyone tensed, expecting fireworks. Instead, he nodded, pointed, and said, "Alright, let's stop right there. Nobody climbs until we fix this. Who tied it off last?" The worker raised his hand. The super nodded again. "Good—thanks for owning it. Let's do it right together." Ten seconds of calm authority taught more than any speech ever could.

That's the subtle difference between compliance and culture. Compliance says, "Do it because you're told." Culture says, "Do it because it's who we are." Accountability turns from enforcement into instinct when it's modeled like that—steady, fair, and consistent.

Transparency strengthens accountability too. Share results. Post safety metrics, inspection outcomes, progress charts. Visibility turns abstract promises into public commitments. When numbers are open, ownership spreads. Nobody wants to be the reason the line dips. Transparency makes accountability communal—it turns leadership from a solo act into a shared mission.

Sometimes accountability will reveal uncomfortable truths about your systems, not your people. Maybe procedures are confusing or tools inadequate. Listen to those signals. Blaming individuals for systemic flaws breeds burnout. True accountability includes fixing the structure around the behavior. When people see you improving the system as well as correcting them, trust deepens.

The best foremen I know do this naturally. They'll say, "If the guys missed the mark, that's on me too—I didn't set them up right." That's leadership maturity. It's an understanding that accountability isn't vertical—it's circular. Every action on the crew ties back to how well the system was built, communicated, and reinforced. Great leaders own the conditions, not just the outcomes.

You can make accountability contagious by recognizing it. When someone steps up to own a mistake, thank them before you coach them. *"I appreciate your honesty. Let's fix it together."* That simple sentence rewards integrity and keeps honesty alive.

And when accountability spreads like that, something powerful happens—your people start self-policing. They begin to see accountability not as management's hammer but as their own code of honor. That's when you know culture has taken root.

Finally, remember that accountability is cumulative. Every small promise kept—every report turned in, every follow-up completed—builds a reputation for reliability. Over time, that reputation becomes culture. Teams stop waiting for reminders because the expectation is self-enforcing. That's when accountability graduates from policy to personality.

Accountability is tested most when things go wrong. It's easy to talk about ownership when the numbers look good and nobody's hurt. The true measure comes when a mistake lands hard and public. What happens next defines your culture.

The weak response is denial or distraction. The strong one is transparency. The moment an incident occurs, gather facts, take action, communicate.

Admit what happened. Outline what you're doing about it. Tell the truth before rumor does. People can forgive failure; they rarely forgive deceit. The more visible you are in those moments, the faster trust recovers.

A few years ago, a project I oversaw had a close call—no injury, but it could have been serious. I called a meeting that afternoon. We reviewed what failed, who was involved, and what we'd missed in our process. There was no yelling. No blame. Just learning. One worker said later, "That was the first time I wasn't scared to tell the truth." That's the moment accountability stops being reactive and starts being cultural.

Recovery always starts with honesty. The first sentence out of your mouth after a mistake sets the tone for everything that follows. If your words sound like an excuse, you lose credibility. If they sound like ownership—*"Here's what I did, here's what I learned, and here's how I'll fix it"*—you gain it back instantly. Accountability is reputation repair done in real time.

Leaders must also be careful not to weaponize accountability. It's a scalpel, not a club. Used well, it removes infection; used poorly, it causes new wounds. Accountability should aim at improvement, not humiliation. The moment it turns punitive, you teach people to hide. The purpose of correction is correction, not revenge.

That's why follow-up matters. If you discipline someone, check back later with coaching and resources. Otherwise, the lesson hardens into resentment. Growth requires context—help them see how fixing the issue improves everyone's safety and performance. When people understand the *why*, accountability stops feeling like punishment and starts feeling like purpose.

Leaders often forget to hold upward accountability as well—managing those above them by delivering honest data and refusing to falsify progress. It takes backbone to say, "We didn't hit the goal because conditions made it unsafe." That kind of truth may cost comfort but buys integrity. Never let numbers outweigh people. A safe zero is worth more than an unsafe hundred.

Upward accountability is the quiet test of integrity. It's easy to preach safety downward, harder to report risk upward. Yet that's the moment when a leader's true loyalty is revealed: to results or to reality. The best leaders protect truth even when it hurts.

Accountability and empowerment are twins. The more ownership you give people, the more accountability you must expect. Empowerment without accountability creates chaos; accountability without empowerment creates resentment. The balance is giving people the authority to make decisions and the responsibility to own them. When workers can correct issues on the spot and report freely, you've built true engagement. They're not waiting for orders—they're acting from shared values.

One of the best examples I've seen came from a crew lead named Marissa. She told her team, "You have the right to stop work anytime you think something's wrong—but if you do, you also have the responsibility to explain what you saw and help fix it." That statement empowered and obligated them simultaneously. It turned accountability into a shared privilege instead of a threat. Her crew became one of the safest and most productive in the company.

That's what accountability does—it transforms responsibility into pride. Once people associate doing right with respect instead of reprimand, you've rewritten the emotional script of your culture. They no longer follow rules; they defend them.

Accountability without excuses also means keeping promises downward. If you tell your people you'll provide better gear, do it. If you commit to reviewing policies, follow through. When leadership breaks its own commitments, the whole system fractures. Words are easy; follow-through is leadership's currency. Each unfulfilled promise devalues that currency until nobody's buying what you're selling.

Small acts of consistency rebuild faith faster than grand gestures. Showing up to the toolbox talk on time, responding to messages, inspecting what you said you'd inspect—these are the micro-transactions that build trust. People watch patterns, not speeches. Accountability lives in the pattern.

You'll also discover that accountability simplifies decision-making. Once the standard is clear and you know you'll own the outcome, choices become obvious. Excuses complicate; ownership clarifies. The mental energy once spent defending yourself is now available for problem-solving. That's why accountable teams work calmer and smarter—they've removed drama from the process.

Sometimes accountability means saying no. No to shortcuts, no to unplanned changes, no to unsafe demands. Saying no when pressure says yes is leadership in its purest form. It's drawing a line between integrity and convenience. The courage to refuse something wrong is the foundation of every strong reputation.

If you lead long enough, you'll face the opposite challenge: holding someone accountable you genuinely like. That's the hardest kind. Friendship tempts leniency. But fairness must outweigh friendship. When you let standards slip for one person, you quietly tell everyone else that integrity depends on personal preference. The kindest act you can offer a friend is honest correction. Respect built on truth lasts longer than comfort built on compromise.

Leaders should celebrate accountability publicly. Recognition reinforces behavior faster than punishment deters it. When someone steps forward and says, "That was my fault," use that moment to model what ownership looks like. "That's how professionals handle mistakes." You're not rewarding error—you're rewarding honesty. That small acknowledgment can transform the fear around accountability into pride.

Leadership AF Lesson:
Excuses protect your ego. Accountability protects your people. Leaders who teach ownership over explanation create teams that move faster, trust deeper, and recover stronger.

A culture without excuses breeds innovation. When people stop wasting time defending failure, they start inventing solutions. Energy once spent on avoidance gets redirected into improvement. Meetings shift from "Who messed up?" to "How do we make it better?" That's when you know accountability has matured into collective intelligence.

Training also plays a role. Teach your supervisors how to give feedback that sticks. Not every leader is naturally skilled at it. Provide examples, role-play

CHAPTER 3: ACCOUNTABILITY WITHOUT EXCUSES

tough conversations, and emphasize empathy. Feedback without empathy is noise; empathy without feedback is neglect. The combination is where growth lives.

Technology can support accountability, but it can't replace it. Apps, checklists, and dashboards track compliance, but human follow-through enforces it. Don't mistake data for discipline. Numbers can tell you *what* happened, not *why*. That's the leader's job—to interpret and act.

A high-accountability culture eventually becomes self-correcting. Crews start coaching each other, supervisors spend less time policing, and everyone feels safer. It doesn't happen overnight. It takes repetition—hundreds of moments where you resist the urge to make excuses and choose ownership instead. Over time, the pattern becomes instinct.

When that happens, accidents drop, performance rises, and trust thickens like mortar between bricks. You've built something stronger than compliance—you've built conscience. People start saying "we" instead of "they." They stop waiting for someone else to fix it because they know they are someone else.

Accountability without excuses is the hinge between words and results. It's where culture stops being talk and becomes truth. It requires humility, courage, and relentless follow-through. It's not glamorous, but it's the reason teams survive storms and rebuild stronger.

Every day ends with a quiet test: *Did I own my part?* If the answer is yes, you've led well. If not, tomorrow's another chance to get it right. That's leadership—an unbroken cycle of ownership and improvement.

And that's the heart of the matter. Accountability isn't a meeting, a form, or a threat. It's a habit of honesty that turns ordinary workers into professionals and managers into leaders. When people see you hold yourself to the same line you draw for them, they stop needing reminders. They start mirroring your standard.

When that happens—when your culture runs on trust instead of fear—you've built something no excuse can survive.

Chapter 4: Consistency Builds Culture

"Anyone can do the right thing once. Leadership means doing it every time."

Consistency is the quiet builder of culture. It's not flashy, not loud, and rarely celebrated, but it is the single most powerful force in leadership. You can have integrity, courage, and accountability in short bursts, but without consistency, none of them take root. Consistency is what turns isolated actions into habits and habits into culture.

A crew doesn't follow what you say once; they follow what you do repeatedly. If your expectations shift with your mood, your people will do the same. They'll chase approval instead of excellence. But when your words and actions match every day—when you're steady regardless of weather, workload, or who's watching—you teach predictability. And predictability is safety. People relax when they know the rules won't change with the wind.

Human beings are wired for rhythm. The brain finds comfort in patterns—it scans for what repeats because repetition means security. Chaos, even subtle chaos, makes people cautious. That's why consistent leaders create calmer, sharper, safer crews. They build environments where attention goes to the task, not to guessing how the boss will react.

Culture isn't created by speeches or posters. It's shaped by repetition—tiny, consistent choices that stack up until they define what "normal" looks like. Every leader has two options: build that normal intentionally, or watch it form by accident. The latter is always messier.

Consistency doesn't mean perfection; it means dependability. It means you

CHAPTER 4: CONSISTENCY BUILDS CULTURE

respond the same way to the same situation, whether it's Monday morning or Friday afternoon. It means your crew can predict your reaction because it's built on principle, not personality. Over time, that steadiness becomes the rhythm of the team. People sync to it.

Early in my career, I worked with a foreman named Curtis. He wasn't loud, but everyone knew where they stood with him. If you did well, he'd say, "Good work, keep it tight." If you didn't, he'd say, "Fix it and do better." That was it. Same tone, same expectation, every time. No rollercoaster. No guessing. Crews loved working for him because they could focus on the job, not his moods. His consistency was a safety feature in itself.

That's what consistency does—it removes confusion. It keeps people focused on performance instead of politics. Inconsistency, on the other hand, breeds anxiety. When rules shift or standards depend on who's watching, people stop thinking about the mission and start thinking about survival. They play defense instead of progress. A leader's inconsistency becomes everyone's distraction.

You can measure the strength of your culture by how it behaves when you're not there. If production drops or safety slips the moment you leave, your presence is management, not culture. Real culture performs consistently even in your absence because your standards have become everyone's reflex. That's the difference between compliance and conviction. Compliance depends on supervision; conviction depends on belief.

Consistency begins with clarity. You can't repeat what you haven't defined. Make expectations simple, visible, and measurable. Then live them out every day. People learn by pattern recognition, not memory. They'll forget what you said by lunch, but they'll never forget how many times you enforced it.

Small habits are the bricks of culture. Starting toolbox talks on time. Checking harnesses before climbing. Logging inspections without being asked. These actions are the rituals that tell your team what matters. When you perform them daily, they stop being tasks and start being identity. That's when safety stops feeling like a rule and starts feeling like pride.

I once visited two job sites in the same week. Both had the same safety binder, same gear, same procedures. One site was tight—ladders tied, harnesses clipped, paperwork neat. The other was sloppy—anchors loose, forms half-filled, ladders leaning wrong. The difference? The first foreman checked those things every morning without fail. The second checked "when he had time." Same policy, different consistency. One site had culture; the other had compliance.

That's the invisible math of leadership: small consistencies multiply into big stability.

Leadership AF Lesson:
Culture isn't built in meetings; it's built in repetition. Every act you repeat teaches your crew what "normal" means.

Consistency is also the antidote to cynicism. Crews have seen promises come and go. They've heard every "safety first" speech from leaders who never left the truck. The only thing that erases cynicism is steady behavior. When your actions outlast your slogans, belief returns. When people see you walking the job site in the rain with the same attention you give on sunny days, they realize your standard isn't seasonal.

Inconsistency, by contrast, erodes everything faster than neglect. One day you enforce tie-offs; the next you overlook them because "we're behind." One day you praise documentation; the next you say "just get it done." Every exception you allow becomes a new rule. Culture doesn't grow in speeches—it grows in the cracks you leave unsealed.

A strong leader understands that consistency starts inside. You can't lead predictably if your own life is chaos. Self-discipline becomes the foundation. Rest, organization, preparation—these aren't luxuries; they're prerequisites for steadiness. A scattered leader produces a scattered team.

The great irony is that consistency looks boring from the outside. There are no fireworks in doing the right thing day after day. But ask anyone who's ever been part of a disciplined, stable team, and they'll tell you: boring is beautiful. Predictable is powerful. Culture thrives on the calm hum of steady excellence.

The secret to consistency is systems. Don't rely on memory or willpower;

CHAPTER 4: CONSISTENCY BUILDS CULTURE

build processes that make the right actions automatic. Checklists, morning briefings, weekly audits—these are the gears that keep standards spinning even when energy dips. Systems protect you from drift. Without them, even good intentions evaporate under pressure.

I once worked with a production manager named Elena. She built her crews around simple, repeatable systems—same pre-task plan every morning, same 10-minute huddle, same sign-off process. It wasn't glamorous, but her division had the lowest incident rate in the company. When asked her secret, she said, "It's not genius—it's rhythm." She understood that leadership isn't about heroic effort; it's about predictable effort.

There's a saying I use in training: *What isn't scheduled doesn't survive.* If you want consistent inspections, put them on the calendar. If you want consistent communication, set daily check-ins. Hope isn't a plan. Schedule is structure, and structure is freedom.

Leaders sometimes worry that too much structure kills creativity. In reality, structure liberates it. When people know the boundaries are solid, they can innovate safely inside them. Consistency doesn't stifle—it steadies. It gives your team a reliable foundation to build on.

Consistency also governs tone. If your communication style shifts from calm to chaotic, people tune out. You don't have to sound the same every day, but your message should. Encouragement, correction, instruction—they should all come from the same place: professionalism. Consistent tone keeps emotions from hijacking clarity.

There's another side to this: consistent follow-up. Starting something strong and then disappearing sends a mixed message. Whether it's a new safety program, a checklist, or a training cycle, consistency in execution is what separates initiatives from fads. People need to see your commitment last longer than the announcement.

I remember a company that rolled out a "Safety Excellence Initiative" with banners, T-shirts, and kickoff meetings. Three months later, leadership had moved on to the next big idea. The crews joked about it for years. That's what inconsistency does—it teaches people to wait you out. Consistency teaches them to join you.

Consistency also creates fairness. When every rule applies equally, morale stabilizes. There's no guessing, no favoritism. People may not like every policy, but they'll respect that it's enforced evenly. Predictability beats popularity. A steady hand earns trust even from those who disagree.

The hardest part of consistency is endurance. Enthusiasm fades; fatigue tempts compromise. The trick is remembering why you started. Every standard exists to keep someone safe, to ensure quality, to uphold integrity. When you reconnect with that purpose, consistency stops feeling like effort and starts feeling like service.

Leadership burnout often comes from inconsistency—trying to motivate through intensity instead of repetition. You don't need to reinvent passion daily; you need to repeat purpose faithfully. Great teams aren't built through adrenaline; they're built through rhythm. A steady beat outlasts any loud performance.

When pressure rises, consistency becomes leadership's compass. Deadlines, inspections, bad weather—they all test whether your standards are situational or absolute. The moment you lower them "just this once," the message spreads: everything is negotiable. The hardest word for an inconsistent leader to say is *no*. The strongest leaders say it often. "No, that shortcut isn't worth it. No, we won't skip documentation. No, safety isn't optional." Every *no* builds

the walls that protect your culture.

Consistency doesn't mean stubbornness. It's not refusing to adapt; it's refusing to abandon your principles while adapting your methods. The goal is progress without compromise. You can change the *how* without betraying the *why*.

The best measure of a consistent leader is memory. Ask any crew member a year later what their supervisor stood for, and if they can answer in one sentence—*"He never let safety slide," "She was fair but firm," "He always showed up"*—you've built legacy. Inconsistent leaders leave confusion; consistent ones leave clarity.

Consistency gives culture its spine, but it also gives leaders peace. Once your standards are stable, decisions come easier. You don't have to debate your values every morning. You've already chosen them. That mental stability

CHAPTER 4: CONSISTENCY BUILDS CULTURE

frees you to lead from purpose instead of reaction.

Momentum in leadership doesn't come from speed; it comes from repetition. Every time you repeat a right behavior, you add one more push to the flywheel of culture. In the beginning, it's heavy. You'll feel resistance. You'll repeat the same reminders until you're sick of your own voice. Then one day, it clicks—the crew starts repeating your words before you do. That's momentum. When the culture starts carrying itself, consistency has done its job.

You can't fake consistency. It's not charisma. It's not slogans. It's daily demonstration. A leader's pattern becomes the organization's pulse. If you show up late, your crew's timing slips. If you cut corners, they'll follow suit. But if you show up early, prepared, calm, and ready, the whole tone of the job changes before a single nail is set. People crave predictability because it builds trust, and trust builds performance.

Consistency doesn't always mean visible action; sometimes it means quiet attention. The act of being present—checking in, walking the site, saying the same few words that reinforce expectation—those small gestures build familiarity. Familiarity breeds confidence. Confidence breeds safety. It's all connected.

I once worked with a superintendent who started every day with the same ritual. He'd walk the perimeter, greet each crew, and ask one question: "What's your plan for safety today?" He asked it so often that after a few months, foremen began answering before he spoke. He didn't need a speech; his presence and repetition said everything. Years later, that site still quoted him. That's legacy built one consistent minute at a time.

Consistency is how you mentor without even realizing it. Younger workers aren't watching what you say—they're watching what you repeat. They're building their version of leadership based on your patterns. If they see you skip the hard parts, they'll think that's acceptable. If they see you hold the line calmly, they'll learn steadiness. Every act of consistency becomes a lesson that outlives you.

One danger every seasoned leader faces is complacency disguised as consistency. It's easy to confuse steadiness with stagnation. The goal isn't to keep doing the same things mindlessly; it's to keep doing the right things intentionally. Review your systems. Refresh your methods. Keep the standards fixed but the tools flexible. Evolution and consistency can coexist if you remember the difference between principle and procedure. Principles rarely change. Procedures should improve.

Consistency also drives communication. When updates come regularly—weekly reports, monthly reviews—rumors shrink. Uncertainty feeds anxiety; steady information starves it. Even bad news hurts less when it arrives on schedule. People can prepare for predictable impact, but they panic in surprise. Regular, transparent communication is leadership's anxiety medicine.

Sometimes consistency is as simple as finishing what you start. Halfimplemented programs, forgotten initiatives, and broken promises create cultural noise. People start thinking, *This will pass like all the others.* Don't let that happen. If you announce a new standard, follow it to completion.

Closure signals seriousness. Every finished cycle reinforces credibility.

Consistency builds resilience. When storms hit—literal or figurative—the teams that survive are those with established habits. They don't have to invent discipline mid-crisis; they already live it. Their processes keep them steady while others scramble. The calm isn't accidental—it's the dividend of months of repetition.

There's a concept called *muscle memory* in both training and psychology. The body learns by repetition until reaction becomes automatic. Leadership works the same way. When you practice consistency long enough, integrity becomes instinct. You no longer have to choose to do right; it simply feels wrong to do otherwise.

Another benefit of consistency is that it multiplies efficiency. Routine reduces decision fatigue. When everyone knows the drill, fewer words are needed. Meetings get shorter, corrections faster. The organization starts running on rhythm instead of reminders. That rhythm frees leaders to focus on growth instead of firefighting.

The most underrated form of consistency is gratitude. Recognizing good work shouldn't be occasional—it should be routine. A simple "Nice job on the setup" every single day does more for morale than a once-a-year award ceremony. People remember daily encouragement long after they forget formal praise. Gratitude practiced consistently becomes part of the environment; it softens correction because people already feel seen.

Fairness depends on consistency, but so does grace. Correcting someone doesn't mean condemning them. Show the same patience to others that someone once showed you. Consistency in empathy is what turns leaders into mentors. Your people should never have to guess whether today is a good day to ask for help.

Culture often reflects the worst habits tolerated, not the best ones celebrated. That's why you must inspect the routine, not just the results. A clean incident report might hide a growing habit of near misses. Consistent observation catches drift early. You don't need to micromanage—you just need to stay visible.

Leadership AF Lesson:
Your consistency is someone else's confidence. What you repeat becomes their reality.

Over time, consistency matures into identity. "This is how we do it here" becomes more than words; it becomes muscle memory. The power of a culture built on consistency is that it requires less external control. People internalize the mission. They self-correct because they know deviation isn't who they are. That's when you move from management to leadership and from compliance to commitment.

Consistency also simplifies succession. When your standards are built into habits, the next generation inherits clarity instead of chaos. They don't have to reinvent culture; they just have to continue it. The greatest leaders aren't those who make culture depend on their presence—they're the ones who make it survive their absence.

Endurance, not excitement, is the secret ingredient. Consistency is measured in months and years, not moments. Anyone can inspire a crew for a day; only consistency sustains them through seasons. That's why culture isn't a sprint—it's a lifetime of laps around the same core values.

There will be days when repetition feels thankless. When nobody notices your steady hand, remember that consistency isn't performance—it's investment. Culture compounds like interest. The reward doesn't appear instantly, but when it does, it's exponential.

Keep showing up. Keep saying the same truths. Keep reinforcing the same standards. Boredom today is safety tomorrow.

And when someone asks how you built such a reliable team, you'll smile and tell them the truth: *"One consistent day at a time."*

That's the essence of leadership's fourth lesson. Integrity starts the culture, courage defends it, accountability sustains it—but consistency keeps it alive. It's the quiet drumbeat beneath every great crew, every safe job, every thriving company. The rhythm never changes because the mission never does.

Do it right. Do it again. And again. Until the doing becomes the knowing. That's how consistency builds culture—and how culture, in turn, builds legacy.

Chapter 5: Communication Is Leadership's Superpower

"Words build worlds. Every conversation shapes the culture you walk into tomorrow."

Communication is the oxygen of leadership. Without it, everything suffocates—trust, morale, performance, safety, and progress.

It doesn't matter how much knowledge you carry, how solid your plans are, or how impressive your credentials look on paper. If you can't communicate clearly, calmly, and consistently, you can't lead. Communication is not a soft skill—it's the hardest, sharpest one to master.

Leadership without communication is like a crew without tools. You can shout all day about values and safety, but if your message doesn't land where people live, it never takes root. The difference between a good leader and a great one is their ability to translate vision into understanding. Clarity is what turns orders into ownership.

Communication isn't about volume; it's about connection. A leader's power doesn't come from how loudly they speak—it comes from how deeply they're understood. Your words should bridge, not bludgeon. They should carry intention and direction, not confusion and noise. Every great culture is built on shared language, and every broken one is haunted by what was left unsaid.

Early in my career, I believed leadership meant always having the right thing to say. But experience taught me that great communication starts with listening. Real listening—the kind where you're not just waiting for your turn to talk. You learn things when you stay quiet long enough for people to reveal what they actually think. Listening turns assumptions into awareness, and awareness is what keeps teams from walking into blind spots.

I remember standing on a job site once, halfway through a roof tear-off, when a worker named Frank approached me, frustrated. "Nobody told me we changed the anchor layout," he said. "I tied off the old way like always." I almost corrected him—but then I paused. He wasn't being careless; he was being honest. Somewhere between my last email and the foreman's last meeting, the message had died. Frank wasn't the failure—the system was. That moment taught me something permanent: if the message doesn't reach the hands doing the work, it never existed.

Every word you speak as a leader either builds or breaks trust. You can't separate communication from credibility—they rise and fall together. Promise something and don't deliver, and people stop listening. Dismiss someone's concern, and they stop speaking. But show them that your words mean something, that you follow through, and suddenly, your voice starts carrying weight. They'll start listening even when you're not talking because your actions echo your words.

Communication is leadership's superpower because it multiplies impact. You can only be in one place at a time, but your message can travel anywhere. When a crew member repeats what you said to another worker, when a foreman uses your phrase in a meeting, when your tone becomes their standard—that's how culture spreads. You've created linguistic gravity. Your words start pulling people toward a shared center of purpose.

Clarity is the most underrated leadership tool in existence. A clear message cuts through noise faster than authority ever will. People don't resist direction—they resist confusion. Every instruction that begins with "I thought you knew" is a prelude to an incident report.

One project manager I knew had a saying taped to his desk: "If it can be misunderstood, it will be." It was his daily reminder that clarity takes more effort than assumption. He'd repeat back instructions to his crews: "Here's what I heard—correct me if I'm wrong." He said it every time, and guess what?

CHAPTER 5: COMMUNICATION IS LEADERSHIP'S SUPERPOWER

His sites had half the rework of anyone else's. Clarity saved time, money, and pride.

Leaders who underestimate communication usually confuse talking with leading. But leadership communication is different—it's intentional, directional, and disciplined. You don't just fill silence; you shape it. You give meaning to moments. You turn chaos into clarity.

When stress hits a crew, the loudest voice wins—so make sure it's yours, and make sure it's calm. Communication during crisis defines confidence. If your team sees you speaking clearly under pressure, they'll mirror that composure. Panic spreads fast; so does poise.

In safety leadership, communication is literally life-saving. Think of how many incidents start with a missed message: someone assumed, misunderstood, or wasn't informed. The root cause often isn't negligence—it's noise. When expectations aren't clear, chaos fills the gap. The most powerful hazard control isn't always PPE—it's communication.

Communication is also empathy in motion. It's how you show that people matter beyond their output. Asking, "How's your family?" or "What do you need from me today?" might seem small, but those questions are trust builders. They tell people that you see them, not just their role. Connection first, correction second—that's how influence deepens.

I once saw a superintendent kneel beside a new roofer during a job walk. The worker's hands were shaking slightly from nerves—first week on the crew. Instead of barking instructions, the superintendent said, "Take a breath. We all started somewhere. You're part of the team now—let's walk through it together." That moment did more for that worker's performance than any reprimand ever could. The man stood taller afterward, and by the end of the week, he was the one reminding others to clip in. That's what empathy looks like with a hard hat on.

The challenge is that communication breaks down fast when leaders get busy. We start assuming people "should know by now." But assumption is the silent killer of consistency. Just because you said something once doesn't mean it's understood—or remembered. Repetition isn't nagging; it's leadership maintenance. The best communicators repeat core messages so often that their crews can finish their sentences. That's not overcommunication—it's cultural reinforcement.

Language defines culture more than any policy manual ever will. The words you repeat become the phrases that shape behavior. "Safety first" means nothing if it's just printed on the wall. But when a leader says, "We don't take shortcuts—we take care," and lives it, that phrase becomes a living code. Crews begin to use it with each other, and suddenly, it's not your rule anymore—it's their belief.

A leader's tone sets the emotional temperature of the team. If your tone is sarcastic, defensive, or dismissive, expect that same energy back. If it's respectful, clear, and confident, that's what will echo. Your tone is contagious; it teaches people how to talk to each other. When communication turns toxic, the cure starts with your own voice.

Listening is how you gather information, but asking questions is how you guide it. Great leaders ask questions that open thinking instead of shutting it down. "What do you see here?" "What would make this safer?" "What's one thing we can do better tomorrow?" Those questions pull wisdom from the field that you'd never get from behind a desk. Communication isn't oneway—it's a loop. Ask, listen, respond, repeat. That rhythm keeps
information flowing and problems shrinking.

One of the most dangerous phrases in any organization is "I thought you knew." It's the ghost of bad communication haunting every mishap. If someone didn't know, the system failed. If someone knew but didn't speak up, the culture failed. Either way, communication is the root. Leaders can prevent both by closing every loop: confirm, clarify, and follow up. "You got that?" isn't enough. "Tell me how you'll handle it" confirms comprehension.

Every misunderstanding avoided through clear communication saves time, money, and sometimes lives. Yet, communication is often treated as an afterthought—a "soft skill" that sits behind technical expertise. But leadership lives in the soft stuff. The strongest structures aren't always visible. You can't see trust, respect, or clarity, but you can see their absence in every mistake made without them.

Think of communication as risk management for relationships. It prevents

CHAPTER 5: COMMUNICATION IS LEADERSHIP'S SUPERPOWER

emotional and operational accidents. You can't fix what you don't know, and you won't know if people don't feel safe enough to speak. Creating that safety starts with language—words that invite, not intimidate. When leaders say, "You can tell me anything," and mean it, communication becomes protection, not performance.

Leadership AF Lesson:
Clear communication isn't what you say—it's what they understand.

One of the hardest communication lessons leaders learn is that clarity requires courage. It's easy to talk around truth; it's harder to deliver it cleanly. Sugarcoating weakens your message. People deserve the truth, spoken with respect, not avoidance disguised as kindness. Direct communication isn't cruelty—it's clarity. A worker can fix what they understand; they can't correct what you won't say.

Effective communication also means tailoring your message to the audience. The same point won't land the same way with everyone. The new hire needs detail. The veteran needs purpose. The executive needs perspective. Good communication isn't one-size-fits-all—it's custom-fit to comprehension. You're not dumbing things down; you're breaking things open.

Leaders must also master nonverbal communication—the unspoken signals that speak loudest. Body language, eye contact, posture—these reveal more than any memo. If your face says "I'm too busy," your words don't matter. If your tone says "You're wrong," your message won't land. People read sincerity faster than they hear instruction. To communicate well, your demeanor must match your words.

Miscommunication doesn't just create errors—it breeds stories. When people don't know the truth, they fill in the blanks. Rumors are the vacuum cleaners of leadership silence; they suck up uncertainty and spit out misinformation. The only way to stop that is to stay visible and vocal. When your people hear directly from you, the noise loses power.

The best communicators are translators—they turn complexity into clarity.

They know how to take a policy written in legal jargon and turn it into something a roofer, welder, or warehouse worker can understand and act on. That's not simplification—it's skill. Anyone can read a rule; few can explain it in a way that sticks. Great leaders translate not just language but values, making the abstract concrete.

When communication works, it looks effortless. But behind every simple message is discipline—preparation, awareness, and intention. Leaders rehearse in their heads how to say something before they say it. They know timing matters. The same truth delivered in the wrong moment becomes friction instead of progress. Leadership communication isn't random; it's strategic.

Good communication also protects energy. Confusion drains motivation faster than fatigue. When people don't know what's expected, they waste time guessing. Clear direction gives purpose, and purpose gives endurance. The quickest way to motivate a team isn't pep talks—it's clarity. People work harder when they know where they're going and why it matters.

Feedback is where communication and accountability meet. It's the bridge between awareness and improvement. But feedback done wrong destroys trust faster than silence. Too often, leaders treat feedback like a verdict instead of a conversation. The goal isn't to make someone feel small—it's to make them capable. The best feedback corrects without crushing. It's precise, calm, and focused on growth.

Timing matters just as much as tone. Feedback delivered in the heat of frustration sounds like criticism; delivered with calm sounds like coaching. Don't wait weeks to talk about something that happened today. And don't let emotions speak before wisdom does. A leader's words in those moments can build a future or burn a bridge.

The formula is simple: Describe, don't diagnose. Say what you saw, not what you assume. "You didn't tie off at the ridge" is fact; "You don't care about safety" is judgment. One invites correction; the other provokes defensiveness.

Facts teach. Accusations close ears.

Leaders who communicate well don't just speak—they teach through their words. Every message, whether it's a quick correction or a safety briefing, is a

CHAPTER 5: COMMUNICATION IS LEADERSHIP'S SUPERPOWER

chance to transfer principle. You're not just talking about a single act; you're showing what the standard looks like. When people leave your conversations clearer and more confident, you've done your job.

Great communication also means clarity at every level of the organization. You can't expect consistent results from inconsistent messages. Leadership alignment is key. If a project manager says one thing, a superintendent says another, and a foreman interprets it differently, chaos follows. Everyone must speak the same language. That's how organizations stay sharp and focused. Culture breaks not from what's said but from how many ways it's said.

Internal communication—how departments, teams, and leaders talk to each other—is just as vital as field communication. Gaps between office and site, or between management and crews, create resentment. When workers feel decisions are made in silence, they lose connection to the "why." The cure is transparency. Share reasoning, not just results. When people understand the purpose behind policies, compliance becomes commitment.

The tone of leadership communication defines the health of the environment. Sarcasm, gossip, and negativity from leaders create toxins that spread fast. What you tolerate in conversation becomes the soundtrack of your culture. A good rule of thumb: if you wouldn't want your words played back in a team meeting, don't say them. Leadership maturity is measured by conversational discipline.

Communication is also the tool that turns conflict into collaboration. Differences in opinion aren't threats; they're opportunities for clarity. Avoiding tough conversations only compounds confusion. Addressing them directly, with respect, builds unity. Disagreement handled well creates stronger understanding. It's not harmony that makes teams great—it's honest communication under pressure.

When you're dealing with conflict, focus on the issue, not the individual. People can change behaviors when they feel valued, but they dig in when they feel attacked. "We need to fix this process" is collaborative. "You keep messing this up" is confrontational. Your phrasing decides whether the conversation becomes progress or a power struggle.

Emotional intelligence turns communication into connection. The ability to read the room, sense stress, and adjust your approach separates leaders from bosses. If your team is overwhelmed, this isn't the time for a lecture. If morale is low, it's the time for empathy, not authority. The best communicators know when to speak, what to say, and when to stay quiet. Presence is sometimes louder than words.

Consistency in communication builds reliability. When you speak predictably and follow through on what you say, people start trusting your word as truth. They'll listen to short memos, brief reminders, or quick texts because they've learned that your communication always carries value. Inconsistent communicators lose influence one broken promise at a time. Every ignored question, every delayed update, chips away at trust.

Leadership AF Lesson:
In chaos, the calmest voice leads.

Remember, communication doesn't end with your words—it continues with your follow-up. A message without follow-up is noise. You have to confirm that what you said turned into what they did. Otherwise, you're managing assumptions, not performance. Verification is part of communication. It's how talk becomes truth.

Clarity also comes from simplification. Leaders sometimes drown people in details. Complexity doesn't make you sound smarter—it just makes you harder to follow. The art of leadership communication is distillation: saying the most with the least. The clearer the message, the stronger the execution.

Leaders must guard against noise fatigue—when people stop hearing because communication has become cluttered. Too many announcements, too many slogans, too much talking without listening. Simplify the flow. Make every communication moment count. Quality over quantity. When your words always matter, people stop tuning out.

The highest form of leadership communication is inspiration through authenticity. People know when you mean what you say. When your stories are real, when your language sounds like you, not like a corporate script, they'll listen. Authentic communication doesn't require fancy vocabulary. It requires honesty, passion, and purpose. Speak from the field, not from a podium.

Leadership communication is also legacy. Long after you've moved on, your words will still circulate in the culture. The phrases you repeat—your sayings, your standards, your tone—will echo in meetings you'll never attend. Every great leader leaves behind a language. Choose yours carefully. It will outlive your title.

If you strip leadership down to its most essential element, it's communication. Every vision needs words. Every standard needs instruction. Every relationship needs understanding. Without communication, leadership collapses into assumption and noise.

Communication isn't just something leaders do—it's what they are. It's the bridge between integrity and influence, between expectation and execution, between people and performance. It's the daily act of shaping reality through words.

The best leaders aren't the ones with the most authority; they're the ones who create the most clarity. Communication is leadership's superpower because it multiplies every other strength. Integrity, courage, accountability, consistency—they all depend on how well you communicate them.

Speak with purpose. Listen with intent. Repeat with patience.

That's how words become culture. That's how communication becomes leadership.

Chapter 6: Recognition, Gratitude, and the Power of Appreciation

"People work for a paycheck, but they give their best for pride."

Recognition is leadership's secret fuel. It costs nothing, yet it powers everything—loyalty, morale, performance, and safety. When leaders notice effort, people give more of it. When they don't, energy drains. You can have the best systems, the sharpest tools, and the most detailed procedures, but if people feel invisible, excellence disappears quietly.

Recognition isn't about ego-stroking. It's about acknowledgment—saying, *I see you, and what you do matters.* Every human being wants to feel significant. That need doesn't vanish on a jobsite; it intensifies. Roofers stand in wind and rain, installers sweat through summer heat, foremen juggle deadlines. A simple "Good work today" can anchor them when the hours feel endless.

True recognition is precise. "Nice job" is noise; "The way you managed that steep pitch safely and still hit production shows real discipline" is leadership. Specific praise shows that you're paying attention. It tells your team that excellence isn't invisible, that you notice details the same way you expect them to.

Recognition also reinforces the behavior you want repeated. What you praise, you multiply. If you highlight safety compliance more often than speed, you shift values. If you celebrate the worker who reports a near miss instead of hiding it, you teach that honesty matters more than image. Leadership communication isn't just corrective; it's reflective—it mirrors the culture you want.

Leadership AF Lesson:
Recognition turns values into habits.

Gratitude transforms recognition from a transaction into a connection. Saying "thank you" isn't weakness; it's respect. The best leaders don't reserve gratitude for big wins—they scatter it through ordinary days. They thank the worker who checks anchors without being told, the admin who catches an error, the driver who returns equipment spotless. Each "thank you" builds invisible equity.

Gratitude also protects humility. The moment leaders believe success belongs only to them, they lose touch with the people who make it possible. Gratitude keeps you grounded. It reminds you that leadership is built on service and shared effort, not status.

There's a story I'll never forget. A crew member once told me he left a company not for pay, but because no one ever said thank you. He'd worked twelve years, never missed a shift, trained new hires, and left quietly one Friday. His supervisor found out Monday. "I didn't even know he was unhappy," he said. But unhappiness isn't always loud. Sometimes it's silence where recognition should've been.

The irony is that recognition isn't hard—it just requires intention. The leader's greatest resource is attention. Wherever you direct it, energy grows. If you only focus on what's wrong, you'll breed fear. If you focus on what's right, you'll breed pride. Pride is contagious. Crews that take pride in their work self-police their safety. They don't wait for inspection—they inspect each other.

Recognition also sharpens accountability. People who feel appreciated don't hide mistakes; they correct them. When leaders treat success as a shared victory, failure becomes a shared lesson. Gratitude creates psychological safety—the invisible net that lets people take responsibility without fear of humiliation. That's how teams mature.

Appreciation isn't a perk; it's performance management done right. Studies in every industry confirm what intuition already knows: people perform better for leaders who notice them. But appreciation must be authentic.

Empty praise sounds like management. Genuine appreciation sounds like mentorship. The difference lies in effort. You can't fake sincerity for long.

Leaders sometimes say, "I shouldn't have to thank them—they're just doing their job." But that mindset misses the human point. Yes, it's their job—but it's also their pride, their sweat, their hours away from family. Gratitude doesn't reward the task; it honors the person behind it. Recognition says *you did it*; gratitude says *you matter*.

Safety culture, especially, runs on appreciation. The more you celebrate proactive behavior—someone stopping work to fix a hazard, someone speaking up about a concern—the more those actions become normalized. Recognition removes the stigma from caution. You turn safety from a rule into a reputation.

There's an art to public versus private praise. Public recognition builds morale; private appreciation builds loyalty. Use both. In meetings, highlight collective wins—"This crew completed three months incident-free." In private, pull someone aside: "You've been a steady hand on this team; your consistency sets the tone." That second one plants roots.

When you lead with gratitude, you stop micromanaging. Appreciation shifts focus from control to trust. You start seeing your people as partners, not problems to fix. Trust grows where recognition flows.

Leadership AF Lesson:
People repeat what earns respect.

The hardest thing about recognition is remembering to do it when times are tough. Stress blinds leaders to small victories. But that's when appreciation matters most. In chaos, morale depends on acknowledgment. Even when budgets tighten and timelines squeeze, gratitude costs nothing. A calm "I know it's been a grind, but your professionalism hasn't gone unnoticed" can steady an entire crew.

Recognition must also be equitable. Favoritism poisons culture faster than criticism. Praise should be earned, not distributed by personality. Measure performance, not popularity. People can accept strict standards if they're applied fairly. Recognition without fairness feels like manipulation; recognition with fairness feels like truth.

Appreciation also travels upward. Leaders forget to recognize their own mentors, coordinators, and executives. Gratitude shouldn't flow only downhill. When respect moves in all directions, communication opens. Everyone feels responsible for the atmosphere. A culture of recognition feeds itself.

Finally, gratitude is a habit that outlasts motivation. Motivation fades; gratitude renews. Leaders who practice daily appreciation never run dry because they're constantly reminded of the good surrounding them. It keeps perspective fresh. Leadership without gratitude becomes entitlement.

Leadership with gratitude becomes legacy.

Recognition isn't about gifts or gimmicks. It's not pizza parties or plastic trophies. Those things might make people smile for a moment, but they don't create pride. Pride grows from purpose. Real recognition happens when someone's effort connects to the mission—when they see that what they did moved the whole team forward. That's why the best recognition is specific, timely, and personal.

Appreciation that lands has three traits: **it's noticed, it's named, and it's necessary.**

- **Noticed:** You saw it happen. You were paying attention.
- **Named:** You can articulate exactly what mattered and why.
- **Necessary:** You made it clear that what they did was essential to the bigger picture.

That combination turns a simple "thank you" into leadership currency. The more you spend it, the richer the culture becomes.

You don't have to turn recognition into a program to make it effective—you just have to make it normal. When appreciation becomes routine, it no longer feels staged. The goal isn't to create one big "employee of the month" moment; it's to build a thousand small ones every week. Culture doesn't grow in ceremonies; it grows in habits.

Recognition also works as a diagnostic tool. If you can't find anything to praise, it might not be your team that's the problem—it might be your attention. Leaders who only see mistakes are like critics who never create. You can't inspire improvement by only highlighting what's broken. The best leaders fix issues without erasing the person behind them. They balance truth with encouragement, precision with perspective.

Gratitude strengthens teams in ways metrics never will. It softens edges, opens communication, and turns compliance into commitment. When people know they'll be appreciated for doing things right, they stop hiding when things go wrong. They engage, report, and correct because they trust they'll be treated with respect. Gratitude creates psychological safety, and psychological safety drives performance.

One morning, I visited a crew that had gone six months without a safety incident. I brought coffee and donuts—nothing fancy, just acknowledgment. I thanked them for setting the standard and asked what they thought contributed to their streak. One guy said, "We just look out for each other, man." Another added, "Yeah, and we don't get chewed out when we call stuff out." That's the heart of it. Gratitude had created confidence. Accountability had become mutual.

When leaders express genuine appreciation, it also breaks down barriers. Hierarchies shrink when humility enters the room. A CEO thanking a laborer for consistent attendance says more about the company than any mission statement ever could. When everyone feels seen, everyone contributes differently. Gratitude isn't weakness—it's leadership strength disguised as kindness.

Recognition can also recalibrate a burned-out culture. When fatigue sets in, the first casualty is enthusiasm. People stop volunteering ideas, stop caring about details. That's when gratitude does its best work. Remind them that what they do matters beyond numbers. "Your attention to detail is what keeps families safe." That one sentence can reignite purpose faster than any incentive.

CHAPTER 6: RECOGNITION, GRATITUDE, AND THE POWER OF...

Leaders sometimes think gratitude has to be grand, but consistency beats extravagance every time. A small, daily word means more than an occasional speech. Think of it like sunlight: a little every day sustains life; too much at once just burns out. When appreciation becomes part of your natural communication, you stop needing reminders. It becomes reflexive, not reactive.

Practical recognition systems don't have to be complex. Keep it human. Write short notes. Mention names during meetings. Create a "caught doing it right" board. Encourage peer-to-peer recognition. Recognition doesn't lose power when shared—it multiplies. The best recognition cultures aren't leader-driven; they're team-powered. Everyone watches for good work because they know it'll be valued.

There's also a secret benefit: recognition strengthens observation. When you start looking for good work, you start noticing it. You train your eyes to see more than risk—you see resilience, craftsmanship, teamwork. It balances your focus and keeps you from falling into cynicism.

Leaders who express gratitude consistently build cultures that self-correct. Teams in those environments don't wait for a manager to enforce standards—they take ownership because they care. Gratitude turns rules into values. When someone says, "We don't work like that here," that's appreciation echoing through culture.

Recognition also builds retention. Paychecks keep people hired; appreciation keeps them loyal. Workers who feel valued stay longer, speak better of the company, and recruit others who share their values. Turnover costs vanish when belonging replaces burnout. You can't buy that kind of loyalty—you build it with words.

Leadership gratitude even extends to conflict resolution. When you start a tough conversation with acknowledgment, defenses lower. "I appreciate how dedicated you are, but we need to fix this part." That's balance. People can absorb correction when it's wrapped in respect. Recognition doesn't cancel accountability; it amplifies it. It tells the truth with grace.

Gratitude also has long memory. The worker you thank today might be the leader you rely on tomorrow. Every time you recognize someone's effort, you plant a seed for the next generation of leadership. When they start leading, they'll remember how it felt to be seen—and they'll repeat it. That's how culture sustains itself.

The power of appreciation is cumulative. Each expression of thanks, each word of recognition, adds to an invisible account that pays dividends during hard times. When mistakes happen or stress peaks, that balance of trust softens the blow. People give grace to leaders who've given gratitude.

Recognition also works on leaders themselves. Practicing gratitude rewires your perspective. It reminds you that leadership isn't a burden; it's a privilege. The more you focus on what's good, the more resilience you gain. Complaints shrink when gratitude grows.

At the end of every week, take a minute to reflect—not on what went wrong, but on who went right. Write down three names. Reach out to those people. Text them. Tell them why they mattered. That's leadership maintenance. It keeps you human, humble, and hopeful.

Gratitude is contagious. When people see appreciation modeled from the top, they mirror it across the team. Crews start thanking each other. Departments stop blaming and start cooperating. The tone shifts. That's how gratitude scales—it moves from practice to culture.

Leadership AF Lesson:
Gratitude doesn't need a reason—it creates one.

In the end, recognition, gratitude, and appreciation aren't separate ideas. They're three expressions of the same truth: people need to feel valued. Recognition says, *I see you.* Gratitude says, *I'm thankful for you.* Appreciation says, *You make a difference.* When those three flow together, workplaces stop feeling like jobs and start feeling like missions.

Leadership is human work. Tools wear out, policies change, but the way you make people feel stays permanent. The crew might forget your meetings, your metrics, even your rules—but they'll never forget how it felt to work for someone who saw them, thanked them, and believed in them.

Recognition is more than a gesture—it's the foundation of belonging. Gratitude is more than politeness—it's the language of leadership. Appreciation is more than emotion—it's evidence of respect. Together, they create cultures that thrive long after the leader moves on.

Lead with gratitude. Speak appreciation. Recognize excellence often and loudly.

That's how you build trust that never fades. That's how you lead like you've got a pair.

Chapter 7: The Standard You Walk Past Is the Standard You Set

"The moment you stay silent in the face of wrong, you've taught everyone watching that wrong is acceptable."

Every culture is defined not by what leaders preach, but by what they permit. The standard you walk past—the behavior you ignore, the shortcut you excuse, the corner you allow to be cut—becomes the real rule of the job. It's not the written policy that defines culture; it's the unwritten permission.

When leaders talk about "raising the standard," they usually mean improving performance or tightening accountability. But standards don't rise through slogans—they rise through action. Every day, you set a silent example. You do it with what you enforce, what you tolerate, and what you excuse. People watch what you walk past. They take notes. They learn what you *really* value.

It's tempting to believe that culture is built through big speeches and formal meetings. It's not. Culture lives in the smallest interactions—the five seconds where you choose whether to speak up or look away. The standard you walk past at 8:17 on a Tuesday morning when you see an untied harness or a blocked exit says more about your leadership than any all-hands meeting ever will.

Leadership isn't just about setting expectations; it's about defending them. If you turn your head from a violation because "we're behind schedule,"

CHAPTER 7: THE STANDARD YOU WALK PAST IS THE STANDARD YOU...

you've just rewritten the rulebook for everyone watching. They'll remember that you cared more about speed than safety. You didn't need to say it out loud—they heard it loud and clear in your silence.

Leadership AF Lesson:
Silence is consent in disguise.

Great leaders understand that culture is contagious. It spreads through imitation. If you're consistent, disciplined, and principled, your crew mirrors those traits. But if you let one thing slide, you've given permission for ten more. Culture never drifts upward. It only decays when left unattended.

That's why leadership requires vigilance. You can't inspect once and assume compliance forever. You can't call out one mistake and then relax. Standards survive only through constant reinforcement. Every walk-around, every conversation, every correction keeps the edges sharp. Neglect dulls them faster than negligence.

The standard you walk past also applies to attitude. Disrespect, gossip, and negativity rot culture just as fast as unsafe acts. When someone mocks a coworker or shrugs off responsibility, that's not harmless—it's cultural erosion. If you laugh along or say nothing, you've silently endorsed the behavior. And soon, others will follow.

I once worked with a supervisor who prided himself on being "easygoing." He said, "I pick my battles." But over time, his crew started picking their rules. Ladders went untied. PPE disappeared. The language on site turned toxic. When I asked why, one of his workers said, "Because he doesn't care." The truth hurt because it was earned. The supervisor didn't need to say he didn't care—he showed it by what he walked past.

The hardest part of leadership is holding the line when nobody else will. It's easy to call out problems when the cameras are rolling or upper management is visiting. But integrity happens in the shadows—in the ordinary, unglamorous moments when doing the right thing costs time, comfort, or popularity.

Walking past mediocrity might save you five minutes today, but it costs you months of credibility tomorrow. Once people learn that standards are negotiable, they'll negotiate them constantly. A single unchallenged violation becomes a new baseline. That's how great cultures collapse—not through one disaster, but through a thousand silent allowances.

Holding standards doesn't make you harsh; it makes you honorable. It means you care enough to protect people from the slow slide into complacency. The goal isn't perfection—it's presence. People don't expect leaders to catch everything, but they do expect leaders to care enough to try.

When you see something wrong and act, you teach everyone watching that accountability is alive. You remind them that standards matter because people matter. When you walk past it, you teach that convenience matters more. Every ignored hazard or disrespectful act tells a story about your priorities.

There's a quiet moral weight to leadership. When you put on that title—foreman, supervisor, manager—you inherit responsibility for more than results. You're responsible for the example. You can't demand excellence from others while accepting average from yourself. That contradiction breeds resentment. People may not confront you about it, but they'll copy you, and that's worse.

Leadership AF Lesson:
People don't rise to your expectations—they fall to your example.

Some leaders claim, "I don't want to be the bad guy." But accountability isn't about being the bad guy—it's about being the right one. If your crew respects you, they'll take correction, even if it stings. What they can't respect is inconsistency. Fair correction earns loyalty; selective silence earns distrust.

The phrase "The standard you walk past is the standard you set" applies far beyond safety. It governs ethics, communication, and integrity. When you let a lie slide because it's small, when you let disrespect slide because it's "just joking," when you let shortcuts slide because "it's just this once," you're rewriting your organization's character one exception at a time.

Leadership isn't built on grand gestures—it's built on micro-moments.

You're setting standards in every handshake, every email, every decision about whether to speak or stay silent. The strength of a culture is measured by how often its leaders refuse to look away.

There's a story I tell often. During a site visit years ago, I saw a worker on a roof without his harness tied off. I stopped the job immediately. The foreman said, "We're almost done up here." I said, "Then you're almost done being in compliance." That moment set the tone for months. The crew understood that we don't measure safety by convenience. The standard held, and morale improved. Why? Because people trust what leaders enforce.

Every time you correct something, you're not being difficult—you're being dependable. People might groan in the moment, but deep down, they respect leaders who mean what they say. Consistency builds confidence.

Inconsistency builds chaos.

The standard you walk past also affects mental culture. If you let burnout fester or ignore signs of stress, you're teaching that exhaustion is normal. Leaders who never acknowledge fatigue create teams that hide it until it breaks them. You can walk past unsafe mindsets just as easily as unsafe acts. Both are dangerous.

Leaders must train their eyes to see both—the physical and the psychological. The blocked ladder and the burned-out foreman are both hazards. If you walk past either, you're setting a precedent that suffering in silence is part of the job. That's not leadership—it's neglect dressed as toughness.

Walking the standard means embodying it. You can't enforce what you don't practice. If you want punctuality, be early. If you want safety, gear up. If you want honesty, tell the truth even when it hurts. Hypocrisy is leadership's loudest failure. People will forgive mistakes, but they won't forgive double standards.

Culture doesn't need another speech—it needs another example. Every leader says "safety first," but few mean it when the schedule tightens. The real test of leadership isn't the priority you preach; it's the one you protect under pressure.

Leadership requires moral courage—the kind that doesn't need an audience.

It's the quiet decision to correct what others ignore, even when nobody else will back you up. It's the steady voice that interrupts the shrug and says, *No, that's not who we are.* Moral courage doesn't shout; it stands. And every time you stand for something right, the standard rises a little higher.

The standard you walk past also shapes your reputation. Long after a job ends, people remember the moments when you chose principle over popularity. They might not remember every meeting or memo, but they'll remember that you spoke up when it mattered. You didn't let things slide. You stood your ground. That kind of leadership leaves a scent—it lingers in the air long after you've walked away.

Every leader faces a choice between comfort and conviction. Comfort whispers, *It's not that big a deal.* Conviction answers, *It's always a big deal.* Because it is. When you start compromising on the small things, you lose the strength to hold the big ones. Integrity erodes one silent approval at a time. And when you finally need your standard to mean something, it won't. It'll be too late.

A lot of leaders mistake tolerance for kindness. But kindness without accountability isn't compassion—it's avoidance. The kindest thing you can do for a worker is hold them to a high standard. That's respect. Low standards aren't merciful; they're insulting. They tell people you don't believe they're capable of better. When you walk past poor performance, you steal the chance for someone to rise.

Leaders who hold the line consistently discover something profound: enforcement creates freedom. The clearer the boundaries, the less confusion. Teams don't waste energy guessing what's allowed—they already know. They trust the rules because they've seen them lived. And trust turns into confidence. Confidence turns into performance.

The standard you walk past defines your leadership legacy. You can have a long career and still leave nothing behind if your example was weak. But even a short time in leadership can echo for years if you were known for your consistency. People won't remember how fast you worked, how many jobs you managed, or how many meetings you ran—they'll remember what you refused to walk past. They'll remember what you stood for when standing was uncomfortable.

The deeper truth is that leadership isn't about policing—it's about protecting. You're not enforcing standards for the sake of control; you're doing it to keep people safe, proud, and professional. The standard protects everyone. It keeps the strong from becoming careless and the new from being overwhelmed. When enforced fairly, it becomes the great equalizer.

I've seen cultures transform when leaders stopped walking past small issues. Crews that used to shrug at safety checks started running them before being asked. Supervisors who once stayed in the truck started walking sites again. The tone changed. It wasn't fear that created it—it was clarity. People finally knew what mattered and believed it wasn't negotiable. That's when the job became safer, smoother, and more efficient all at once.

Even so, enforcing standards doesn't mean becoming rigid. Flexibility is essential for problem-solving, but it must never cross into moral compromise. A good leader knows when to adapt methods and when to protect meaning. You can bend procedures for improvement, but you never bend principles for convenience. Every leader must know that line—and defend it fiercely.

Some of the best leadership moments are invisible. The quiet correction, the private talk, the split-second decision to turn around instead of walking past something wrong—those are the moments that separate leaders from bystanders. Nobody will applaud you for them, but they're the foundation of every great culture. Leadership often looks boring because consistency doesn't sparkle. But consistency saves lives, protects dignity, and builds empires that last.

People are always watching. Not because they're judging, but because they're learning. They're studying how leadership behaves under pressure, what you'll ignore, and where you'll act. They're not listening for your words—they're waiting for your reaction. Every look away is an unspoken lesson. Every act of courage is one too.

When you refuse to walk past something wrong, you're not just protecting a standard—you're protecting the future. The apprentice watching you today will be the leader enforcing those same expectations tomorrow. You're teaching them what "normal" should mean. Every standard you defend now becomes the inheritance of the next generation.

The worksite is a reflection of leadership. If it's clean, disciplined, and respectful, leadership is too. If it's sloppy, dangerous, and negative, leadership probably walked past a few too many things. The roof, the warehouse, the boardroom—it's all a mirror. You can see your leadership staring back at you in the condition of your environment.

The standard you walk past is not just a workplace truth—it's a life truth. It applies at home, in friendships, and in how you treat yourself. If you walk past your own unhealthy habits, your own procrastination, your own neglect, those become your personal standards. You're not exempt from your own rule. Every choice shapes your example, and every example shapes your world.

Leadership doesn't start with authority; it starts with awareness. The best leaders aren't just looking for what's wrong—they're paying attention to what's right. They catch both, correct one, and encourage the other. They don't walk past excellence either; they recognize it. Holding standards isn't only about stopping bad behavior—it's about honoring good behavior with equal intensity. That balance keeps morale high and culture stable.

The day you stop walking past things that don't meet the mark, you become the kind of leader others wish they had. You become the mirror of excellence that people look into to improve themselves. You become the reason safety meetings feel sincere, the reason accountability feels fair, and the reason culture feels alive.

Every great leader eventually learns that words fade, policies expire, and systems evolve—but standards endure. Standards are immortal. The ones you defend outlive your name. The ones you ignore outlive your excuses.

The standard you walk past is the standard you set—always. Not sometimes. Not when it's easy. Always. Because leadership is never neutral. Every silence is a statement, and every action is a sermon.

Lead by what you stand for. Speak up for what matters. Protect the standard that protects your people.

Because in the end, that's not just leadership—that's legacy.

Chapter 8: Leading Through Adversity

"Anyone can steer when the seas are calm. Leadership begins when the storm hits."

Adversity doesn't build character; it reveals it. Every leader will face moments where plans fail, pressure mounts, and the easy options vanish. Those are the moments that separate managers from leaders, and talkers from doers. You don't discover what kind of leader you are when things go right—you discover it when everything goes wrong.

Adversity is leadership's mirror. It reflects what you truly believe, not what you say you believe. When the schedule falls apart, when tempers flare, when safety is tested, and everyone's looking at you for the next move—your reaction defines the culture. Chaos reveals conviction.

Most people want leadership to be linear—a checklist of actions and rewards. But adversity breaks that illusion. Real leadership is messy. It's walking into a storm you didn't cause and deciding to stand tall anyway. It's making decisions with incomplete information and limited time. It's staying calm when everyone else panics, not because you're fearless, but because your fear isn't in control.

Pressure doesn't invent character; it amplifies it. Whatever values you've built in quiet seasons will scream under strain. If you've practiced consistency, patience, and integrity, those qualities will carry you through chaos. If you've relied on charm, shortcuts, or authority, adversity will expose that, too. Hard times test whether your leadership is built on foundation or façade.

One of the hardest truths about adversity is that it doesn't discriminate. It comes for everyone. Equipment fails. Weather turns. A trusted employee quits. A project goes sideways. Adversity is part of the job description, but how you handle it becomes your reputation. The best leaders aren't those who avoid problems—they're those who absorb them without losing control of their principles.

Leadership through adversity starts with emotional discipline. The first instinct under pressure is reaction—raise your voice, assign blame, panic. But leadership requires response, not reaction. Reaction is instinct; response is intention. The space between the two is where wisdom lives. That's where you decide whether the situation controls you or you control yourself.

When a leader loses composure, the entire team mirrors it. Panic trickles down faster than direction. But composure works the same way. If you can stay steady—measured words, even tone, clear instructions—your people will borrow your calm until they can find their own. Leadership isn't about pretending you're unshakable; it's about being stable enough to help others stand when they can't.

Adversity also tests communication. In chaos, clarity is the most valuable tool you have. People don't need motivational speeches; they need direction. Tell them what's happening, what's next, and what you expect. If you don't fill the silence, fear will. When uncertainty takes over, rumor becomes reality.

Communication during crisis isn't optional—it's oxygen.

There's a story I often tell. A few years ago, we were facing a jobsite shutdown after an unexpected inspection. Emotions ran high. Some blamed management; others wanted to rush and hide mistakes. But leadership meant stepping forward, not hiding behind excuses. I gathered the crew and said, "Here's the truth: we missed a step. We'll own it, fix it, and move forward the right way." The tone shifted instantly. People relaxed because they had direction. Honesty defused panic. Leadership through adversity doesn't mean being flawless—it means being transparent.

Leaders who vanish during adversity lose trust forever. The moment your people can't find you when things go wrong, they'll stop believing you when things go right. Adversity is the time to show up—not to delegate, not to disappear, but to demonstrate. Even if you don't have all the answers, your presence says, *we're in this together.* That's the kind of leadership that sticks.

Leadership AF Lesson:
Adversity doesn't destroy leaders—it exposes the ones who were never leading.

Adversity also reveals the health of your culture. Teams that rely solely on authority crumble when pressure hits. Teams built on trust endure. In healthy cultures, people don't freeze—they act, communicate, and adapt. They're not waiting for orders; they're operating from shared values. That's why leaders must build resilience long before the storm. You don't prepare for adversity in adversity. You prepare in routine, in discipline, in consistency. The storm just shows whether your preparation was real.

Another trap leaders fall into during hardship is isolation. They think, *I'll deal with this alone.* But isolation kills clarity. You need perspective, support, and accountability. In adversity, lean on your mentors, peers, and team. Asking for input isn't weakness—it's strategy. A leader who listens under pressure doubles their intelligence instantly.

Leadership through adversity is also about empathy. When people are afraid, they don't need orders—they need assurance. They need to know their leader sees them as more than tools. Simple gestures—a hand on a shoulder, a direct "we'll get through this"—carry weight that spreadsheets never will. Adversity is when leadership becomes personal.

Even so, empathy without direction is chaos. People still need a plan. The best leaders balance both: compassion and command. "I know this is tough, but here's our next step." That's leadership language under pressure—truth first, plan second, encouragement third. Anything else feels hollow.

Leaders who thrive in adversity are the ones who stay purpose-driven. They don't ask, *Why is this happening to me?* They ask, *What can I learn from this?* That mindset shift changes everything. Every challenge becomes an opportunity to refine systems, strengthen communication, and deepen trust.

Adversity can't be avoided, but it can be leveraged.

Leaders who treat adversity like a teacher grow stronger every time it returns. They stop fearing the storm because they've learned to read the wind. Every obstacle becomes another page in their leadership training manual. The more they face, the calmer they become. Eventually, the storm becomes familiar—not comfortable, but manageable.

Resilient leadership also requires vulnerability. Pretending you're unaffected by stress doesn't inspire anyone. It creates distance. When you're honest—when you say, "Yeah, this is tough, but we'll push through"—you connect. Authenticity under pressure builds respect. Nobody trusts the leader who claims to be bulletproof; they trust the one who bleeds and still keeps going.

Adversity also tests fairness. Pressure tempts leaders to play favorites or assign blame unevenly. But adversity is when fairness matters most. When you treat everyone equally—even when it's hard—you reinforce unity. Your people might disagree with your decisions, but they'll respect your integrity if it's consistent.

Finally, adversity demands reflection. After the storm passes, the best leaders don't just move on—they analyze. They ask, "What did we learn? Where were we weak? What worked?" That reflection turns pain into process. Every setback becomes data. Every mistake becomes a manual for the next challenge.

Adversity may bruise, but it shouldn't break. It should build. That's how seasoned leaders emerge—not because they avoided failure, but because they faced it head-on and learned to use it.

Adversity isn't just a stress test for systems—it's an x-ray for leadership. It exposes cracks that comfort concealed. The truth is, smooth sailing never forged greatness. Nobody grows in the sunshine; they grow in the storm. The pressure, the uncertainty, the long nights—these are the furnaces where resilience and authenticity are tempered into strength.

When adversity hits, the leader's job isn't to eliminate difficulty but to navigate through it. That means learning to regulate your emotions, control your narrative, and protect the tone of your environment. People can handle almost anything if they believe their leader won't crumble. Leadership during crisis is emotional stewardship—you set the thermostat for everyone else's courage.

Resilient leaders know that adversity is temporary, but how you act during it is permanent. You may not remember the exact details of every tough season, but you'll always remember how you showed up. More importantly, so will everyone who followed you through it. Adversity doesn't define your people's faith in leadership; your response does.

When things go wrong, the first question from a strong leader isn't, "Who messed up?" It's, "What can we fix right now?" That shift in language transforms chaos into clarity. It tells the team the goal isn't blame—it's recovery. Blame divides; focus unites. Recovery starts the moment leadership refuses to lose its head.

Even the best leaders experience fear and frustration in adversity. The difference is that they've learned to carry those feelings with discipline. They don't unload their stress on their people or make the crew responsible for their emotions. They channel that energy into motion—one decision at a time, one correction at a time. Adversity rewards forward motion. Stagnation is where failure festers.

When you lead through hardship, transparency becomes your best ally. Admit what you know. Admit what you don't. People respect honesty more than false confidence. The phrase "I don't know yet, but we'll figure it out together" is more powerful than pretending to have all the answers. That sentence builds trust because it carries both humility and assurance.

Leaders also have to manage fatigue—both theirs and everyone else's. Adversity drains stamina. That's when consistency matters most. Keep the routines intact. Keep the meetings short but steady. Keep the communication flowing. Familiar rhythms anchor people when the world feels unstable.

It's easy to underestimate how much hope matters in adversity. Hope isn't blind optimism—it's disciplined belief. It's the decision to keep moving, to keep caring, and to keep expecting that effort will pay off even when the outcome isn't clear. Leaders who hold onto that kind of hope give others permission to do the same.

Adversity also changes your perspective on leadership success. It strips away illusions and leaves behind what's real. Titles, accolades, and comfort fade fast when pressure hits. What remains is character, communication, and commitment. These are the only currencies that survive the crash. When everything external burns away, those are the assets that rebuild from the ashes.

The leaders who rise through hardship are the ones who stay teachable. They don't waste time defending their pride. They ask questions, seek advice, and admit mistakes quickly. The faster you own your errors, the faster you evolve. Adversity punishes arrogance but rewards humility.

I've seen leaders lose good people because they couldn't admit they were wrong during a crisis. Pride barricades progress. Humility opens doors. When a leader says, "That one's on me," it doesn't weaken authority—it strengthens it. It shows humanity. It models accountability. And it frees everyone else to be honest, too.

When the storm finally breaks, leadership's job isn't to celebrate—it's to rebuild. People come out of adversity changed. Some are stronger, others are scarred. Rebuilding means tending to both. Debrief honestly. Talk about what hurt and what helped. Make changes. Learn. Growth without reflection is just repetition with new mistakes.

Leadership AF Lesson:
Adversity builds leaders; reflection keeps them wise.

There's a temptation after surviving a crisis to relax, to assume the hardest part is over. But that's when complacency sneaks in. True leaders use the calm to reinforce what the chaos revealed. They repair weak systems, clarify communication, and recognize the people who stood strong. Gratitude after adversity cements loyalty like nothing else.

Leading through adversity isn't glamorous. It's exhausting, humbling work. But when you stay steady, communicate honestly, and lead with heart, people remember it forever. Years later, when your name comes up, someone will say, "He never lost his cool. She never gave up on us." That's the legacy adversity writes for those who refuse to fold.

The storms don't stop coming. They just start shaping you instead of

CHAPTER 8: LEADING THROUGH ADVERSITY

shaking you. Each one makes you sharper, calmer, more compassionate, and more capable of leading others through theirs. You stop fearing adversity because you realize it was never the enemy—it was the instructor.

The real danger isn't failure; it's forgetting what failure taught you. Every challenge carries a lesson. Every storm brings a skill. Adversity gives you experience you can't buy and wisdom you can't borrow. It toughens your edges without hardening your heart—if you let it.

And one day, when you're guiding someone else through their first real test, you'll see the reflection of all your storms in their eyes. You'll know exactly what to say because you've lived it. You'll steady them not with advice, but with presence. You'll show them, by example, that adversity doesn't end leadership—it reveals it.

Because in the end, leadership isn't proven in prosperity. It's proven in pressure. The titles fade, the comfort fades, but character endures.

So when the next storm comes—and it will—stand tall. Don't curse it. Lead through it. The people around you aren't looking for a superhero; they're looking for someone who stays human, focused, and unbreakable.

That's leadership through adversity.

That's how you lead like you've got a pair.

Chapter 9: From Compliance to Commitment

"Rules control behavior; belief changes it."

The difference between a rule follower and a culture builder is belief. Compliance happens when people do the right thing because someone's watching. Commitment happens when they do it because they believe it's the right thing to do—even when no one's around. The goal of leadership isn't just to get people to follow the rules; it's to help them care enough that they don't need the rules to act right.

Compliance keeps you out of trouble. Commitment keeps you excellent. One is about obedience. The other is about ownership. Compliance follows policy; commitment follows purpose.

A compliant worker wears their harness because the foreman says so. A committed one wears it because he wants to go home to his kids. The act is the same, but the motivation is completely different—and motivation is what determines whether safety becomes a rule or a reflex.

Leadership's highest calling is to turn rules into reflexes. That transformation doesn't come from enforcement alone; it comes from engagement. People must see themselves in the purpose of the rule. They need to feel part of something larger than regulation. When they understand the "why," the "how" takes care of itself.

Leadership AF Lesson:
Rules tell people what to do. Purpose tells them why it matters.

CHAPTER 9: FROM COMPLIANCE TO COMMITMENT

Too many organizations stop at compliance because compliance is measurable. It's easy to count checklists, audits, and completed forms. But what can't be measured is often what matters most—trust, integrity, pride, belief. You can't count commitment, but you can feel it. It shows up in the way people speak, the care they take with their work, and the way they look out for each other.

Compliance says, "Don't break the rule." Commitment says, "Don't break our trust." That shift from rule enforcement to relational responsibility is the heartbeat of culture. It's what turns supervision into self-management. When people move from *have to* to *want to*, leadership has done its job.

But this doesn't happen by accident. Commitment must be cultivated. It grows from consistent communication, fairness, and authenticity. People follow what they believe, and they believe what they experience. If you say one thing and do another, you teach compliance—people will mimic your behavior only when forced. But when your words and actions align, you invite belief.

One of the biggest reasons companies struggle to create culture is that they mistake enforcement for leadership. Enforcement works on paper; it doesn't work on people. You can't threaten someone into pride. You can scare them into silence, maybe even obedience, but never into ownership. Fear produces compliance; belief produces commitment.

Compliance may keep you in line, but it doesn't make you care. Caring comes from connection—when people feel seen, respected, and part of something that matters. A leader's role isn't to police behavior but to inspire belief. That's the shift from control to culture.

When you walk a jobsite where people operate from commitment, you can feel it immediately. There's a rhythm—steady, efficient, confident. Conversations are respectful. Equipment is cared for. Pride lives in the details. Nobody needs a speech because the standard has become second nature. That's when you know you've crossed the line from compliance to commitment.

Leaders who live this principle understand that rules are necessary, but they're not sufficient. You can't build culture by enforcement alone; you build it through example, consistency, and shared purpose. The rules are the bones; belief is the muscle. Without both, the body of culture can't stand.

Compliance makes people check boxes. Commitment makes them check each other. A compliant culture does the minimum; a committed one does the maximum without being asked. That's the difference between surviving and excelling.

The challenge is that compliance feels faster. It's easier to say, "Do it because I said so," than to take the time to explain the why. But leadership is a long game. The time you invest in helping people understand purpose pays dividends in safety, quality, and loyalty. Compliance expires the moment supervision leaves; commitment endures long after you do.

In a safety meeting, compliance sounds like rules; commitment sounds like values. Rules say, "Wear your PPE." Values say, "Protect each other." Rules demand; values invite. People resist demands but respond to invitations. When you invite someone to care, you elevate them from a task to a purpose.

Commitment also changes how people see leadership itself. When workers are only ever corrected, they associate authority with punishment. But when they're encouraged, listened to, and included in problem-solving, they see leadership as partnership. They stop working for you and start working with you.

That's the magic shift—from power to participation. A leader's voice stops sounding like control and starts sounding like inspiration. And once people feel inspired, they don't need a rulebook to know what to do. They already believe in doing it right.

There's a story I remember from early in my career. A foreman named Luis ran a crew that consistently exceeded safety expectations. When I asked him how he did it, he said, "I tell my guys the truth—this isn't about the company; it's about our families. I don't want to be the one who has to tell someone's wife that her husband isn't coming home. So, we do it right. Every time." That's commitment in action. His crew didn't need threats or reminders—they shared his conviction.

Commitment can't be mandated. You can't force someone to care. But you can model it until it spreads. That's why leaders who lead from the front build belief faster than those who lead from the office. When people see you living the values, they stop seeing them as rules—they see them as reality.

The path from compliance to commitment begins with one question: *Why do we do this?* If you can answer that clearly, you can teach commitment. If you can't, you'll always default to control. The "why" fuels the "how." Without it, your systems might work temporarily, but they'll never sustain under pressure.

The power of belief also transforms accountability. In a compliant culture, people report out of obligation. In a committed one, they report out of integrity. They correct each other, not to score points or impress a supervisor, but because they care about the outcome. That's ownership—and ownership is the ultimate form of safety.

When you see commitment in action, you see people performing at their best because they want to, not because they're told to. And that kind of motivation doesn't burn out. It doesn't need constant supervision because it's rooted in pride, not pressure.

Commitment doesn't just change results—it changes relationships. Teams that operate from belief communicate better, trust deeper, and handle adversity faster. They stop hiding mistakes and start fixing them together. They don't need a compliance officer to tell them how to behave—they've internalized the standard.

Leaders often ask, "How do I get my people to care?" The answer is simple: show them that *you* care first. Care is contagious. People reflect the energy you project. If you're indifferent, they will be too. But if you lead with conviction, consistency, and heart, they'll match it—maybe even exceed it.

Commitment doesn't happen by accident—it's built intentionally, layer by layer, moment by moment. It's the product of consistent example, honest conversation, and fairness that never wavers. Leaders can't inspire commitment by standing above people; they earn it by standing beside them. A committed team doesn't need daily motivation speeches—they're fueled by shared values. When people understand that the work they do matters, not just to the company but to the community and to one another, effort transforms into pride. Pride, when directed with purpose, is the most powerful safety mechanism on earth. Pride doesn't forget PPE. Pride doesn't cut corners. Pride doesn't need supervision—it's supervision of the soul.

Leaders who operate from a foundation of belief understand that their job isn't to enforce rules but to nurture responsibility. You're not just teaching people *what* to do; you're shaping *who* they become through their work. That's a sacred kind of leadership—it transcends compliance and touches identity. When work becomes part of someone's integrity, commitment is permanent.

Transitioning a culture from compliance to commitment doesn't happen overnight. It takes relentless consistency. Every time you reinforce the "why," you lay another brick in the foundation of belief. Every time you walk the talk, you prove the principle. And every time you celebrate someone who embodies the standard, you make it contagious.

But here's the uncomfortable truth: you can't convert everyone. Some people will always resist commitment because commitment requires vulnerability. It asks for belief—and belief requires trust. If trust has been broken too many times in the past, it takes patience to rebuild it. That's where leadership persistence matters. You keep showing up. You keep living it out. You keep proving that the standard isn't optional, but it is personal.

When people see that your expectations never change with the weather or the workload, they start to relax into trust. They stop wondering whether today's rule will apply tomorrow. They start believing in the consistency behind your leadership. And belief, once earned, becomes the anchor for everything else.

The beauty of commitment is that it creates self-correcting culture. In compliant environments, you need constant oversight. In committed environments, the team polices itself—not out of fear, but out of pride. They protect the culture because they helped build it. That's the invisible magic of leadership done right.

To reach that point, leaders must give up control without giving up standards. That means replacing command with collaboration. Ask more, tell less. Involve your people in decision-making. Ask for their insights on improving safety, efficiency, and morale. When they contribute to the

CHAPTER 9: FROM COMPLIANCE TO COMMITMENT

process, they buy into the outcome. You can't expect commitment from people who've never had a voice.

Commitment thrives in environments where people feel heard. Listening isn't weakness—it's reinforcement. It shows people that their experience matters and that leadership trusts their judgment. When employees feel that respect, they begin to act like owners. And owners don't need constant reminders—they take initiative.

Here's a simple truth: people support what they help create. If you want a committed culture, let your team help shape it. They'll protect what they built. They'll enforce the standard with pride instead of resentment. That's how accountability turns into unity.

The next piece of the puzzle is recognition. Commitment grows in the soil of gratitude. When people see that their effort and care are noticed, they do more of it. Recognition isn't about trophies or bonuses—it's about being seen. It's about the moment you stop and say, "I noticed how you handled that situation—that's leadership right there." Recognition reinforces belief. It's how values become visible.

Leaders often underestimate how small acts of appreciation multiply commitment. A word of thanks, a moment of eye contact, a pat on the shoulder—all of it tells people that their work isn't invisible. That's how you grow commitment: not by shouting rules, but by whispering truth into the spaces where effort lives quietly.

Commitment also demands fairness. Nothing kills belief faster than hypocrisy. If you enforce rules on some and overlook others, you've just chosen compliance over culture. Consistency is the backbone of trust. It doesn't matter if people like every rule; what matters is that they believe the rule applies to everyone equally—including leadership.

Leadership AF Lesson:
You can't preach what you won't practice and expect anyone to believe you.

Sustaining commitment means turning moments into systems. Every success story, every example of pride, every moment of accountability needs to be documented, shared, and celebrated. People forget what they're told, but they remember what they've lived. Capture those moments of belief and turn them into your culture's folklore. Tell the stories that remind your team who they are when they're at their best.

Culture is storytelling with evidence. Every time you celebrate a foreman who stood up for safety, every time you highlight a crew that refused to rush a job, you're saying, "This is who we are." That narrative becomes a mirror your people can look into and see pride staring back.

Over time, commitment becomes the default. You won't need to talk about "buy-in" because the buy-in already happened. The rulebook becomes a safety net, not a leash. People operate from values because they've internalized them. That's when culture shifts from dependent to dynamic—from something enforced to something embodied.

And when new employees arrive, they won't have to be told what the culture is—they'll feel it. They'll sense it in the way the veterans carry themselves, in the way problems get solved, in the respect that flows both ways. That's the power of a truly committed organization. It's not built on compliance; it's built on conviction.

Leaders who master this shift become more than supervisors—they become culture architects. They stop asking, "How do I make them care?" and start asking, "How do I show them it matters?" Once you lead from that place, your influence expands beyond any title or position. You become a multiplier of belief.

Commitment doesn't erase mistakes—it redeems them. When people are committed, they don't hide errors; they learn from them. They don't fear discipline; they welcome feedback. The conversation changes from "Who's at fault?" to "How do we improve?" That's how growth replaces guilt and accountability becomes aspiration, not anxiety.

Commitment also transforms safety culture into life culture. When people carry those same standards home—buckling their seatbelt, checking their equipment, treating others with respect—you've done more than lead a team.

You've changed lives. You've turned compliance into conscience.

And that's the ultimate goal of leadership—not to make people follow the rules, but to help them become the kind of people who live by them naturally.

Rules fade, posters tear, slogans get forgotten. But belief—belief endures. Because belief doesn't live in a binder; it lives in the heart.

The move from compliance to commitment is the evolution of every great culture, every great team, every great leader. It's the moment when rules become reflex, effort becomes pride, and leadership becomes legacy.

That's the mark of a leader who doesn't just enforce standards but inspires them.

That's what it means to lead like you've got a pair.

Chapter 10: Empowering Others to Lead

"Leadership isn't about holding power. It's about handing it over and watching others rise."

The true measure of leadership isn't how many people follow you—it's how many people you help become leaders themselves. The highest form of influence isn't control; it's cultivation. You can tell everything you need to know about a leader by what happens when they're not around. Do people panic, stall out, and wait for instructions? Or do they step forward, take ownership, and keep things moving? That's the difference between a manager and a multiplier—between someone who holds power and someone who gives it away.

Empowering others to lead isn't about letting go; it's about lifting up. It's showing people that leadership isn't reserved for a select few—it's a responsibility that belongs to everyone who cares about the outcome. You don't have to wear a badge or a title to lead. You just have to care enough to make things better and brave enough to take action.

It's one thing to manage work; it's another thing entirely to develop people. When you empower someone to lead, you're planting seeds of confidence in soil that might've gone untouched for years. You're helping them discover strength they didn't know they had. You're not just shaping their performance—you're shaping their identity.

Leadership hoarded is leadership wasted. Every time you clutch authority like it's fragile, you send a message that only one person can be trusted with decisions—and that person is you. But leadership is not meant to be guarded;

it's meant to be given. The strongest leaders build others up to the point where the team doesn't collapse when they step out. They build teams that run on principle, not presence.

Empowerment begins with trust. You can't expect someone to act like a leader if you treat them like a liability. Too many supervisors mistake control for quality. Control feels safe because it reduces surprise, but it also reduces growth. Micromanagement is leadership's silent killer—it suffocates initiative. You can't expect people to take ownership when every move they make is second-guessed.

When you trust someone, you're not saying, "I know you'll never make a mistake." You're saying, "I trust you to learn from the mistakes you will make." That difference changes everything. Because trust doesn't guarantee perfection; it guarantees progress. And progress is what builds leaders.

Micromanagement builds robots. Empowerment builds thinkers.

Empowering others doesn't mean disappearing or tossing responsibility like a hot potato. It means walking beside them, not in front of them. It's giving them room to make choices while knowing you're close enough to catch them if they stumble. That balance between freedom and accountability is the sweet spot of growth.

You're not handing them the wheel and jumping out of the car—you're letting them drive while you're still in the passenger seat, calmly pointing out the road ahead. They'll drift sometimes, hit bumps, maybe even stall the engine. But every trip builds skill. Eventually, they'll drive better than you, and when they do, that's not a threat—that's your success story.

Empowerment is teaching people to solve problems without waiting for rescue. Every time you swoop in with the answers, you're robbing them of a chance to learn. The best leaders don't tell—they ask. Questions like: "What do you think?" or "How would you approach it?" ignite critical thinking. It's not about getting the "right" answer—it's about strengthening their process.

Good questions build independence. And independence is what turns followers into leaders.

Leadership development is an act of patience, and patience isn't passive—it's disciplined restraint. Watching someone fumble through a decision you could've made in five seconds takes maturity. You'll feel that urge to jump in, to fix, to control. But if you do, you're robbing them of the lesson. Just like muscles grow through tension, leadership grows through trial.

When you empower someone, you're not saving them from failure—you're teaching them how to face it. Because sooner or later, failure comes for everyone. The difference between those who break and those who build is how they respond. Empowerment means being there not to prevent the fall but to help them rise after it.

And let's be honest—empowering others is hard. It demands humility. It means you have to stop seeing yourself as the hero and start seeing yourself as the builder of heroes. It's not about how much light you can shine; it's about how many others you can hand the torch to.

There's a quiet kind of pride in watching someone you developed outshine you. It's bittersweet, sure, but it's beautiful. When you see someone handle a problem with poise, communicate with confidence, and lead with compassion—all traits they learned from you—that's legacy in motion.

The truth is, insecure leaders can't empower anyone. They're too busy protecting their image. They confuse importance with irreplaceability. But real leaders know the goal isn't to be needed—it's to be *useful*. When you empower others, you're building something that can last without you. That's not weakness—that's immortality.

One of the most dangerous beliefs in leadership is, "It's faster if I just do it myself." Maybe it is today—but it's slower forever. Every time you do someone else's job, you're building dependency, not capability. Empowerment takes more time upfront because it's an investment, but it pays dividends that multiply.

Think of it like compound leadership. Every person you pour into carries your influence into places you can't go. They take your lessons, your values, and your example with them. You become part of their leadership DNA. But if you never develop them, your influence dies the day you clock out.

Empowering others also means teaching them to lead under pressure. It's easy to lead when things go right—it's a test of courage when they don't.

When your team sees you stay calm in chaos, they learn composure. When

CHAPTER 10: EMPOWERING OTHERS TO LEAD

they watch you own mistakes, they learn integrity. When they feel your trust in them during tough calls, they learn courage. Empowerment isn't just about handing over authority—it's about transferring mindset.

You don't empower people with speeches—you empower them with example.

And sometimes, the most powerful form of empowerment isn't telling someone they're capable—it's showing them through responsibility. Real empowerment feels like pressure at first. It's uncomfortable. It stretches people. But that's where transformation begins. Nobody grows in comfort.

People become leaders not when they're ready, but when someone believes in them enough to say, "Try."

When you tell someone, "You've got this," it might sound small to you, but to them, it's fuel. Belief is the oxygen of potential. And when you give that belief freely, people start seeing themselves the way you see them—capable, trustworthy, valuable. That's when real leadership development begins.

Empowerment also demands clarity. You can't empower people into confusion. It's not enough to say, "Lead." You have to define what good leadership looks like in your culture. What values should guide decisions? What principles matter most? Without direction, empowerment becomes chaos. But when people understand the "why," they can navigate the "how."

The clearest sign of empowerment done right is initiative. When people start anticipating instead of reacting, when they bring ideas instead of excuses, when they take ownership instead of orders—that's empowerment in full bloom.

When I walk onto a jobsite and see foremen who've trained their crews to think for themselves—to spot hazards, to check anchors, to communicate without being told—I know empowerment has taken root. You can feel it. The energy is different. People move with purpose, not pressure.

Empowerment doesn't make things easier; it makes things better. It replaces dependency with dignity. It turns the "Why didn't someone tell me?" mentality into "I already took care of it." And that shift is what transforms workplaces from reactive to proactive.

Leadership AF Lesson:
When you share leadership, you don't lose power—you multiply it.

The world doesn't need more managers—it needs multipliers. A manager measures production; a multiplier multiplies people. One adds results; the other builds revolutions. You can't multiply through fear or control. You can only multiply through trust and teaching.

Empowerment isn't a management tactic—it's a moral obligation. If you hold knowledge, experience, or authority, you have a duty to pass it on. Leadership isn't meant to be a throne; it's meant to be a table. Everyone deserves a seat if they're willing to learn, contribute, and lead.

When you empower people, you unlock parts of them they didn't even know existed. You give them permission to be bold. You give them space to fail. You give them tools to succeed. You help them discover that leadership isn't about being in charge—it's about being accountable.

And when empowerment becomes part of your culture, leadership stops being rare. It becomes normal. It becomes expected. That's when you know you've built something that will outlast you.

Empowering others to lead also transforms how you view control. The old-school mentality says, "If I want it done right, I have to do it myself." But empowerment says, "If I want it done *right again and again*, I have to teach someone else how." That shift changes everything. You stop being a bottleneck, and you start being a builder.

When leaders cling too tightly to control, they become the very obstacle they're trying to avoid. Progress slows down because no one can move without permission. People stop thinking creatively and start doing only what's required. The organization becomes a machine of compliance instead of a movement of commitment.

Empowerment breaks that cycle. It turns tasks into ownership, followers into decision-makers, and workers into leaders. When people feel that their voice matters and their judgment is trusted, they start to care about outcomes on a deeper level. They begin leading not for credit, but for pride.

Empowerment is contagious. When one person feels trusted to lead, they

CHAPTER 10: EMPOWERING OTHERS TO LEAD

naturally pass that trust on to others. They start mentoring, guiding, and inspiring the next wave. Before long, leadership stops being a hierarchy and starts becoming a network—a living, breathing organism made up of leaders at every level.

I once visited a crew that proved this perfectly. The foreman had been with the company for years, known for his calm leadership and consistency. He wasn't loud or flashy—just steady. One day, a storm delayed work, and the foreman got stuck offsite. By the time he returned, the team had already adapted, reorganized, and implemented the day's plan without missing a beat. Nobody waited for instructions. Everyone knew the priorities, the safety steps, and the standard. They didn't need direction because they'd been empowered with purpose.

When I asked the foreman what he thought of their initiative, he just smiled and said, "That's the goal." That's leadership done right—when your people no longer need your constant direction because they're carrying your discipline within them.

Empowerment is slow to build and quick to crumble. You can't fake it. You can't hand someone a little trust one week and take it back the next. Consistency is what solidifies it. If you say you trust your team, you have to show it—especially when things get tough. When pressure hits, the instinct to control creeps back in. You want to grab the wheel, correct the course, and tighten every screw. But empowerment means holding steady. It means trusting the process you built, even when it wobbles.

That's the test of real leadership—whether you trust your people when your own reputation is on the line.

When you empower others, you're not saying, "I'm stepping back because I don't care." You're saying, "I believe in you enough to let you take this." And when they succeed, you celebrate them publicly. When they fail, you protect them privately. That's how you earn loyalty that no paycheck can buy.

Empowerment is equal parts courage and compassion. Courage to let go, compassion to guide through mistakes. Too many leaders default to punishment when something goes wrong. But punishment kills confidence. Coaching builds it. When people fail under your leadership, that's not a cue to humiliate—it's a cue to educate. You say, "Let's figure out what went wrong and what we'll do differently next time." That conversation builds strength far deeper than a reprimand ever could.

If you want empowered people, you have to give them a safe space to grow. You can't cultivate leadership in fear. Nobody experiments when they're afraid. Nobody innovates when they're bracing for criticism. But when people know that mistakes won't destroy them, they take risks. They learn faster. They care more.

There's a difference between recklessness and responsibility, and empowerment helps people find that balance. You're not saying, "Do whatever you want." You're saying, "Take ownership. Think it through. Do what's right." When people understand the mission and the values, they make better choices than you could ever script for them.

That's the quiet genius of empowerment—it replaces micromanagement with meaning.

Empowering others also changes your relationship with recognition. Insecure leaders hog it. Empowered leaders hand it out like oxygen. Every time you give someone credit, you reinforce their confidence. You're telling them, "You did this, and it mattered." Those small acknowledgments fuel big momentum. Because people who feel valued keep showing up with value.

And here's something most leaders miss: empowerment doesn't just benefit your people—it strengthens you. When you delegate responsibility and trust others to carry it, you gain perspective. You free up mental space to focus on strategy instead of survival. You stop reacting and start leading.

Empowerment is the difference between working *in* the system and working *on* the system. The former keeps you busy; the latter keeps you relevant.

The key is humility. You can't empower others if you need to be the smartest person in the room. If your ego requires constant validation, you'll never release control long enough to let others grow. Humility lets you see leadership as stewardship, not ownership. You don't own your position—you're borrowing it for a while, and your job is to leave it stronger than you found it.

CHAPTER 10: EMPOWERING OTHERS TO LEAD

That mindset shift is what separates good leaders from great ones. Good leaders want to be needed. Great leaders want to be missed for the right reasons.

Leadership AF Lesson:
The best leaders don't create followers—they create leaders who create more leaders.

Empowerment is an act of legacy. It's planting seeds you may never see grow. You might never get the credit, and you have to be okay with that. Legacy leadership isn't about applause—it's about impact. The reward isn't being remembered by name; it's knowing your influence still lives on in the decisions, behaviors, and standards of those you developed.

If you want to future-proof your organization, start developing replacements today. Not just one or two, but everyone. Give your people a sense of ownership that outlives your presence. Empowerment is succession planning in motion. It ensures that the lights stay on and the mission keeps moving, even when the faces change.

I've seen the other side too—leaders who refuse to empower anyone because they think no one can do it "like them." Those teams burn out fast. When the leader leaves or falters, the whole structure collapses because nobody else knows how to lead. That's not leadership—that's dependency.

Empowerment is what prevents that collapse. It creates leaders at every level who can think, decide, and act according to shared values. It makes the system flexible instead of fragile.

There's a humility that comes with building people stronger than yourself. It's not always comfortable. You'll feel invisible sometimes. You'll pour effort into someone who doesn't thank you. You'll be misunderstood. And you'll be tempted to pull the power back to prove you're still in charge. Don't. That's your ego talking. Empowerment demands endurance.

Leadership that lasts isn't about being seen—it's about being felt.

Empowerment also changes accountability. When leadership is shared, accountability becomes collective. Everyone starts owning outcomes. There's no "their fault" or "my job." It's *our* standard. And that's when a culture becomes unstoppable—when people hold each other to high standards because they care too much to let things slip.

Empowerment redefines success. It's no longer about how much you did—it's about how much you enabled. The best compliment a leader can ever receive is hearing that things ran just as smoothly without them. That's not a loss of importance—that's proof of effectiveness.

You'll know empowerment has taken root when your absence doesn't create chaos—it creates confidence.

There's a moment in every leader's journey when they realize empowerment is freedom. When you've built people capable of leading themselves, you don't have to control every detail. You don't have to work 16-hour days to keep things afloat. You can step back, strategize, and elevate. Empowerment doesn't just liberate your team—it liberates you.

That freedom also brings responsibility. Because now your role isn't to carry everything—it's to see further, anticipate bigger, and lead longer. Empowerment doesn't make you less essential; it changes *how* you're essential.

There's also a spiritual element to empowerment. When you lift someone else up, you're doing something sacred. You're saying, "I see you. I believe in you. You have value." Those are powerful words in a world where most people are starved for belief. Leadership at its core is an act of faith—faith in others, faith in the mission, and faith that growth is worth the risk.

Empowerment isn't flashy. It doesn't always come with applause. Sometimes it looks like sitting in silence while someone else presents the idea you helped them develop. Sometimes it looks like staying in the background so others can shine. That's okay. Because your reward isn't attention—it's transformation.

Empowerment is also the answer to burnout and turnover. When people feel empowered, they stop seeing their job as "just work." They start seeing it as purpose. Purpose fuels perseverance. A paycheck makes people show up, but empowerment makes them stay—and stay committed.

When empowerment becomes culture, energy changes. You feel it the moment you walk in. People greet each other with purpose. Communication

CHAPTER 10: EMPOWERING OTHERS TO LEAD

flows sideways, not just downward. Initiative replaces excuses. Leadership becomes everyone's business.

In an empowered environment, mistakes are learning tools, not weapons. Feedback is normalized, not feared. Leaders coach instead of command. And people push each other toward greatness because mediocrity feels unnatural.

That's what empowerment does—it shifts normal.

Empowerment is also about timing. You can't just dump responsibility on someone who's not ready and call it "trust." Real empowerment is gradual, guided, and intentional. It's like building muscle—you increase the weight as they gain strength. That's how you avoid breaking people under the weight of unearned pressure.

You start small. You delegate a task, then a project, then a process. You let them run meetings. You let them make calls. You let them make mistakes and talk through the lessons. That's how confidence compounds.

The truth is, empowerment is never done. It's a loop. You empower someone; they grow and empower someone else. That's how cultures of excellence sustain themselves generation after generation.

Empowerment is the purest form of leadership because it's selfless. It's choosing to make yourself smaller so others can grow taller. It's replacing the phrase "I did this" with "We did this." And in the end, that's what defines greatness—not how loud you were, but how many others found their voice because of you.

Empowering others to lead means teaching people to lead even when you're gone. It's ensuring that the flame doesn't go out when your hands are no longer there to hold the torch. It's knowing that leadership, when shared, never dies—it multiplies.

So teach. Coach. Encourage. Listen. Step back.

Trust the people you've built. Let them rise, even if they surpass you. Because if they do, it means you've succeeded in the purest way a leader can.

And one day, when they empower others, your influence will echo in their actions, their words, and their values.

That's legacy. That's leadership.

Chapter 11: The Courage to Correct

"Correction isn't criticism. It's care in motion."

Leadership without correction is a friendship with failure. A leader who can't confront is a leader who can't protect. The courage to correct isn't about authority or control—it's about love. Love for the people you lead, for the standard you represent, and for the future you're responsible for shaping.

Correction is one of the hardest parts of leadership because it's one of the most personal. It's easy to celebrate success; it's harder to confront mistakes. But that's where real leadership lives—not in applause, but in accountability. A leader who avoids correction to stay liked will one day be hated for what they allowed.

The truth is simple: what you don't correct, you condone. Every silence reinforces a behavior. Every time you see something wrong and say nothing, you've told the team it's okay. Correction is uncomfortable, yes, but comfort is overrated when people's safety, trust, and respect are on the line.

Correction requires courage because it risks rejection. People might resist, argue, or walk away. But leaders aren't called to be comfortable; they're called to be consistent. The goal isn't to win every argument—it's to uphold every principle.

When you correct someone, you're not tearing them down; you're protecting them from their lesser self. The best leaders don't correct out of ego; they correct out of empathy. They remember what it felt like to be corrected and how that moment shaped their growth.

CHAPTER 11: THE COURAGE TO CORRECT

Leadership AF Lesson:
If you can't confront someone, you've chosen comfort over culture.

Correction must come from the right heart. If your motive is punishment, you'll lose people. If your motive is growth, you'll gain respect. People can sense intent faster than they can hear words. When correction feels like an attack, walls go up. When it feels like an investment, people listen.

The goal isn't to prove someone wrong—it's to pull them higher. Correction is a bridge, not a weapon. You build that bridge through tone, timing, and truth. Get one of those wrong, and the message collapses before it reaches them.

Tone is your first test. Never correct out of anger. Anger clouds clarity. If you can't correct calmly, wait until you can. Words spoken from frustration might be accurate, but they won't be effective. Correction should feel steady, not explosive—strong enough to be heard but gentle enough to be received. Timing matters too. The middle of chaos isn't the place for confrontation. Correction lands best when it's private, direct, and focused. Public embarrassment breeds resentment, not reflection. The best corrections are done in quiet moments when pride isn't performing.

And then there's truth—the backbone of correction. You can't fix what you won't name. Be specific, be factual, and be fair. Don't exaggerate, don't generalize, and don't lecture. A simple "Here's what I saw, and here's what needs to change" works better than a five-minute sermon. Clarity corrects faster than criticism.

Leadership isn't about catching people doing wrong—it's about helping them do right. Correction should always point forward. If you stop at identifying the problem, you've only done half your job. The second half is guidance: what to do next, how to avoid it, and how to improve.

When you do it right, correction doesn't crush—it builds. The person walks away clear, respected, and challenged, not humiliated. They may not thank you today, but they'll respect you tomorrow. The same people who resist your correction now will often become your biggest supporters later, because they'll remember that you told them the truth when others stayed quiet.

Correction, when done consistently, creates culture. People start correcting themselves before you ever have to step in. They start watching each other, not out of fear, but out of pride. Standards become self-sustaining. But that only happens when correction is fair, consistent, and rooted in care.

Some leaders mistake leniency for kindness. They think being gentle means being permissive. But kindness without correction is negligence. If someone's heading toward a mistake that could cost them their safety, their job, or their credibility, the kindest thing you can do is stop them—firmly, clearly, and early.

You don't wait until someone's at the edge of the cliff to tell them to watch their step. Correction is an act of prevention, not punishment. You don't correct because you want to control someone's choices; you correct because you care about their consequences.

Leadership requires the courage to be unpopular for the sake of what's right. Not everyone will appreciate your corrections in the moment. But leadership isn't a popularity contest; it's a stewardship of trust. Your job is to protect the standard, not the ego.

When you choose not to correct someone because you fear conflict, you've prioritized your own comfort over their growth. And that's not leadership—that's avoidance with a title.

Good leaders don't enjoy correcting; they do it because they understand its necessity. They know that correction today prevents catastrophe tomorrow.

It's easier to mend a mistake than to rebuild a reputation.

The best leaders also accept correction themselves. You can't expect your team to take feedback if you refuse it. Leaders who welcome correction create environments where growth feels safe. They model humility by showing that accountability isn't just for employees—it's for everyone, including the one in charge.

When a crew sees their leader accept feedback gracefully, they stop fearing correction. It becomes part of the rhythm—not a threat, but a tool. The moment people realize that correction is normal and fair, not punitive or personal, is the moment they start learning faster and leading stronger.

Correction also teaches respect. The way you correct someone tells them

CHAPTER 11: THE COURAGE TO CORRECT

everything about your integrity. When you correct with dignity, you teach respect. When you correct with pride, you teach fear. Respect creates growth; fear creates silence.

The courage to correct is the courage to care deeply enough to confront honestly. It's leadership that risks misunderstanding today to protect integrity tomorrow. It's not about being harsh—it's about being honest. Because without honesty, there can be no improvement, no trust, no real leadership.

Correction is not the end of leadership; it's the beginning of learning. The moment after correction is when growth begins—not just for the person corrected, but for the leader, too. How you handle that aftermath defines whether your leadership builds walls or bridges.

After correction, the goal is restoration. The purpose of holding someone accountable is never to shame—it's to sharpen. Once the truth has been spoken and the correction made, you guide them back toward confidence. That's where trust is either lost or earned. When people walk away from correction feeling smaller, you've missed the point. But when they walk away feeling wiser and still respected, you've led them well.

The best leaders know how to follow up. They don't just correct and walk off. They check back in. "How's it going since we talked?" "What's working better?" That second conversation is where credibility grows. It proves that your correction wasn't about power—it was about progress.

Leadership that corrects without following up teaches fear. Leadership that corrects and then coaches teaches strength. People will take correction from someone who's proven they care. That's how correction becomes mentorship—and mentorship becomes culture.

Correction isn't meant to intimidate; it's meant to elevate. You're not fixing a person; you're reinforcing a standard. It's never "You're wrong"—it's "We're better than this." That subtle shift in language changes everything. It turns confrontation into collaboration.

There's no courage in a leader who stays silent when the standard slips. Silence is easy—it's also expensive. The cost shows up later in lost trust, lower morale, and eventually, accidents or failures that could've been prevented. The quiet leader might feel peaceful in the moment, but that peace is just deferred conflict. Real peace comes from knowing you stood up for what's right.

The courage to correct isn't about being fearless—it's about choosing integrity over avoidance. You might still feel your heart race before a tough conversation. That's normal. Courage doesn't cancel fear; it overrides it. Every time you have that conversation instead of walking away, you build a little more muscle in your leadership. And just like physical muscle, that courage grows stronger with repetition.

I've had moments where correction didn't go well—where tempers flared, words got sharp, and egos collided. But even in those rough exchanges, something valuable happened. The air cleared. Truth was spoken. Sometimes leadership means being misunderstood for a while. That's okay. Growth often begins with discomfort.

Correction is an art, not a science. The same words that motivate one person can offend another. That's why tone and relationship matter so much. You earn the right to correct through consistency and fairness. People may not like hearing the truth, but they'll respect it when it comes from someone who's proven they care more about people than politics.

One of the biggest leadership mistakes is assuming that correction ends the moment the words are spoken. In reality, that's when leadership begins. The real test is whether your actions afterward match your message. If you correct someone for cutting corners, and then you cut corners later, you've erased the entire lesson. The follow-through gives correction its power.

Correction is also contagious. When you set the example of addressing issues directly and respectfully, others begin doing the same. It creates a ripple effect. Crew members start having constructive conversations with each other instead of waiting for management to step in. Accountability becomes a shared value, not a top-down directive.

That's when culture truly shifts—when correction is no longer seen as conflict, but as collaboration. A culture that can handle correction can handle anything. Because correction builds resilience, trust, and pride—the foundation of every high-performing team.

When you see a team that never corrects itself, you're looking at a culture

CHAPTER 11: THE COURAGE TO CORRECT

that's dying. It's stagnant, fragile, afraid. But when you see people holding each other accountable—with honesty, respect, and consistency—that's when you know leadership is alive in every corner of the organization.

Leadership AF Lesson:
Correction builds confidence when it's rooted in care.

The courage to correct is also the courage to apologize. Sometimes you'll get it wrong. Maybe you misjudged a situation, overreacted, or missed context. The same humility you expect from your team must live in you. When you say, "I handled that wrong," you're not losing authority—you're gaining authenticity. People don't follow perfect leaders; they follow honest ones.

Correction done right leaves everyone better. The person learns, the team strengthens, and the leader grows. Each correction, handled with care and consistency, adds another brick to the wall of trust. That wall doesn't get built in a day—it's laid one tough conversation at a time.

The truth is, courage doesn't roar in the boardroom. It whispers on the jobsite, in quiet one-on-one moments, when you take a breath and decide to tell the truth. It shows up in the moments when it would be easier to look away but you choose not to. That's where leadership earns its name—not in the title, but in the tension.

The courage to correct also keeps people safe—physically, emotionally, and ethically. It prevents small compromises from becoming big disasters. It protects reputations before they fall apart. It keeps culture honest, and honesty keeps people alive—in more ways than one.

When correction is done right, it becomes one of the most powerful expressions of respect you can offer. You're telling someone, "I see more in you than what you just showed me." That's love disguised as discipline.

The leader who corrects out of love will always outlast the one who avoids out of fear. Because in the end, people want to be led by someone who cares enough to be real. They don't need perfect leaders—they need brave ones.

And bravery doesn't mean shouting louder. It means standing firm, speaking truth, and staying kind. It means protecting the standard when nobody's watching. It means choosing respect over ease.

The courage to correct isn't flashy, but it's foundational. It's what keeps standards alive, cultures strong, and people safe. It's the heartbeat of leadership—steady, strong, and often unseen.

When you lead with the courage to correct, you teach people to lead themselves. You teach them that accountability isn't punishment—it's progress. And in time, they'll start correcting others with the same care you showed them.

That's how leadership multiplies. That's how cultures endure.

Chapter 12: Stay Above the Line

"At every moment, you're either above the line—open, curious, learning—or below it—closed, defensive, and right."

Staying above the line is one of the simplest and hardest disciplines in leadership. It is the line between reaction and reflection, between ego and growth. Every decision, every conversation, every problem places a person on one side or the other. Most rarely notice where they stand until after they have crossed it.

Above the line live curiosity, humility, and accountability. Below the line live blame, pride, and defensiveness. The line is not drawn on the floor—it is drawn in the mind. The purpose is not to remain permanently above it but to recognize when the fall occurs and to rise again quickly. The quality that distinguishes leadership from supervision is not control but recovery: the ability to regain awareness after losing it.

Leaders who remain conscious of this inner boundary understand that awareness is the quiet infrastructure of every organization. It shapes tone, governs decision-making, and decides whether culture becomes toxic or transformative. A company may have perfect systems and still fail if its leaders repeatedly act from below the line. Vision collapses not because people forget the goal but because they forget themselves.

To live above the line requires vigilance. Human instinct prefers the comfort of certainty. When uncertainty strikes, the primitive mind searches for blame. The wiser mind searches for learning. The distinction seems subtle; in practice it defines the health of entire institutions. The belowtheline impulse says, *Who caused this?* The above-the-line perspective asks, *What can be understood here?*

Emotional intelligence turns that curiosity into a tool of stability. The leader who recognizes a rising surge of anger or fear does not suppress it; they translate it. Emotion becomes information: a signal that something matters and deserves attention. In this way, control is not repression but interpretation. Anger points to violated values. Fear reveals uncertainty about capacity. Joy signals alignment. Each emotion, when understood rather than indulged, contributes to wiser leadership.

The pause between emotion and expression is where composure lives. Within that pause, leaders decide whether their reaction will serve the mission or their ego. The gap can be no longer than a breath, yet it contains the entire difference between chaos and coherence. Cultivating that breath—lengthening it until awareness has room to choose—is the daily discipline of mature authority.

When leaders embody this discipline, calm becomes contagious. The tone of one individual regulates the collective nervous system. Teams take cues not from slogans but from the leader's breathing, posture, and word choice. A steady voice turns panic into focus; a reckless tone multiplies confusion. Leadership, in this sense, is less about speaking and more about the quality of silence that precedes speech.

Above-the-line behavior also demands humility. Self-certainty masquerades as confidence, but real confidence is the courage to stay teachable. The leader who can say "I don't know" without shame creates room for others to contribute knowledge. In contrast, the leader who must always be right drives information underground. Ideas cease to flow, and culture hardens into defensiveness.

Organizations that value composure over drama inevitably outperform those addicted to adrenaline. When pressure rises, they do not rush to find culprits; they slow down to clarify facts. Slowness, in this context, is not hesitation—it is precision. Measured response replaces impulsive reaction.

Awareness becomes a form of safety. People trust leaders who remain predictable in their integrity even when outcomes are unpredictable. They know that truth will not be punished. This psychological safety encourages candor, which in turn accelerates problem-solving. Every layer of hierarchy that practices awareness multiplies that effect until it becomes the defining trait of the culture itself.

The process is not mystical; it is neurological. The mind that stays above the line activates the part of the brain responsible for reasoning and empathy. The mind that drops below it activates fight-or-flight reflexes. One opens vision; the other narrows it. Modern organizations operate at the speed of perception—leaders cannot afford tunnel vision.

Awareness also reframes accountability. Above the line, accountability is ownership of influence; below the line, it becomes defensiveness against accusation. The former builds trust because it invites transparency. The latter erodes it because it hides behind explanation. To take responsibility for tone, timing, and emotional impact is to lead with integrity, not apology.

Leadership AF Lesson: Leaders Rise by Choice, Not by Comfort

Rising above the line is not a reflex; it is a decision renewed in every encounter. Comfort encourages repetition; awareness demands intention. The act of choosing presence over pattern is the essence of growth. When leaders govern themselves, they grant others the freedom to govern their own reactions.

Composure becomes collective, not personal.

Sustained awareness is not merely a personality trait; it is a practice of deliberate perception. Leaders who remain steady during turbulence are not inherently calmer than others; they are more rehearsed in awareness. They have trained their attention to linger on what they can control and release what they cannot. That habit, repeated over years, creates a kind of invisible strength.

Composure at that level is not denial of emotion but partnership with it. It is understanding that tension is energy that can either be weaponized or repurposed. When channeled through awareness, tension becomes insight.

When expelled through ego, it becomes collateral damage. The leader who pauses to ask what the emotion is teaching turns volatility into clarity.

The practice of staying above the line transforms not only individuals but also the ethical climate of an organization. The emotionally intelligent leader redefines what accountability means. It becomes less about punishment and more about alignment. People are held responsible not to satisfy authority but to protect shared values. Ethics are upheld not by surveillance but by self-awareness.

A culture rooted in awareness evolves toward integrity almost automatically. When reflection is normal, secrecy has no oxygen. When empathy is rewarded, cruelty becomes socially expensive. In such cultures, policy becomes secondary because behavior is already self-regulating. The organization polices itself not through fear but through conscience.

Below-the-line cultures, by contrast, revolve around control. They produce compliance rather than commitment. They depend on supervision to replace trust. The energy that could fuel innovation instead feeds defensiveness. Meetings become ceremonies of blame disguised as strategy. The cost is invisible but immense: lost creativity, suppressed initiative, diminished joy.

To stay above the line collectively, leaders must build structures that reward awareness. Recognition should follow not only performance metrics but emotional maturity—how calmly a person navigates disagreement, how respectfully they handle correction. These are leading indicators of sustainability. Skills can be trained, but awareness must be cultivated.

The philosophy extends beyond emotional poise to intellectual humility. Awareness protects against the illusion of certainty. In complex systems, every decision carries unintended consequences; above-the-line leaders remain alert to that truth. They do not cling to plans out of pride. They adapt without self-condemnation. Flexibility becomes moral rather than tactical.

In this light, the difference between leadership and management grows clear. Management manipulates external systems; leadership moderates internal ones. A manager adjusts schedules, budgets, and logistics. A leader adjusts energy, perception, and meaning. When leaders remain above the line, every technical skill improves because perspective sharpens.

The philosophical root of the line metaphor lies in consciousness itself.

CHAPTER 12: STAY ABOVE THE LINE

Awareness divides instinct from intention. Instinct acts for survival; intention acts for significance. Evolution may have designed humanity to react quickly, but civilization depends on the few who pause. The ability to think while feeling, to stay centered while being challenged, is what allows progress to exist at all.

This awareness also reframes time. Leaders who live below the line replay the past or pre-fight the future. They rewrite conversations in their heads, defend arguments that have not yet happened. Leaders above the line operate within the present, where information is fresh and agency is highest. Their focus is not scattered among regrets and predictions; it is gathered into precision.

There is also an aesthetic dimension to this mindset. Composure, when genuine, has beauty. It communicates dignity without words. People gravitate toward it instinctively because it signals safety. In a chaotic world, calm is charisma. It does not demand attention; it earns it.

Every generation rediscovers this truth in new language. The Stoics called it equanimity, the Buddhists mindfulness, modern psychology emotional regulation. Whatever the name, the essence remains constant: awareness separates leaders from reactors. Awareness allows intention to outrun impulse.

In practical terms, staying above the line influences how decisions are made. Below-the-line decisions emerge from fear of loss. Above-the-line decisions arise from pursuit of value. One constricts, the other expands. When leaders ask, *What are we protecting?* rather than *What are we avoiding?* strategy shifts from defensive to creative.

This mental altitude also changes how power is perceived. The insecure leader equates power with control. The aware leader sees power as responsibility for energy. They understand that authority amplifies emotional tone. A single careless word from the top can echo through hundreds of lives. Recognizing that weight instills reverence for communication. Words become instruments, not weapons.

The concept of "above the line" also implies perspective. From higher ground, vision extends farther. Problems that seemed insurmountable from below reveal patterns and pathways from above. Awareness grants that elevation. It is not escapism but clarity—rising high enough to see cause, context, and consequence in a single view.

When this discipline matures, it begins to feel less like effort and more like orientation. Leaders stop performing calmness; they become calmness. Their presence steadies others automatically. New employees adjust faster, conflicts resolve quicker, innovation feels safer. Awareness becomes the cultural weather—predictable, clear, sustaining.

Yet vigilance remains necessary. Fatigue pulls everyone downward eventually. Awareness decays without renewal. That is why reflection, rest, and solitude are strategic, not indulgent. They reset perspective. The leader who never pauses eventually mistakes noise for necessity. To stay above the line requires oxygen, both literal and emotional.

Sustained practice also refines empathy. When a leader learns to observe their own mind, judgment of others softens. They see that defensiveness is not defiance but fear. They recognize that arrogance often hides insecurity. This understanding transforms confrontation into compassion without sacrificing standards. People respond not to leniency but to being understood.

The relationship between awareness and accountability thus becomes symbiotic. Awareness provides insight; accountability provides direction. Together they form integrity in motion. A leader who owns their awareness models a standard of humanity that invites respect more deeply than authority ever could.

Awareness, when sustained long enough, evolves into wisdom. Wisdom is simply awareness that has practiced patience. It is perception seasoned by time, self-reflection, and the willingness to admit that understanding will always exceed ownership. Leaders who cultivate that perspective radiate steadiness. They do not demand calm; they generate it.

Over time, an above-the-line culture becomes self-correcting. Teams begin to monitor tone as carefully as output. Meetings feel different—not quieter, but cleaner. Disagreement remains, yet it carries less friction because people have learned to listen for intention rather than ammunition. This atmosphere is not accidental; it is engineered through thousands of small acts of composure.

One of the paradoxes of awareness is that it makes humility visible. The more leaders understand, the more they realize how much remains unseen. That recognition softens communication and strengthens credibility. Employees trust leaders who can say, "I need to think about that." It signals respect for complexity.

In high-performing cultures, humility and high standards coexist. The leader's steadiness sets the range within which everyone else operates. If the leader panics, the team spirals. If the leader breathes, the team recalibrates.

The mathematics of morale are emotional, not procedural.

Awareness also refines courage. Below-the-line courage is noisy—it shouts, defends, and dominates. Above-the-line courage is quiet confidence grounded in clarity. It listens, decides, and accepts consequence without theatrics. This composure under pressure inspires greater loyalty than charisma ever could. People follow stability because it promises safety in motion.

Every system ultimately mirrors its most self-aware member. In families, organizations, even nations, the level of consciousness at the top dictates the level of trust below. When awareness governs action, policies become humane, and expectations become achievable. The inverse is equally true:

when ego governs, fear fills the vacuum.

The mature leader therefore treats self-management as public service. Regulating emotion is not self-help—it is stewardship of influence. Every unnecessary outburst withdraws credibility; every moment of restraint deposits it. Over years, these transactions accumulate into legacy.

Composure also enhances communication precision. Awareness edits words before they escape. It asks, *Is this true? Is it necessary? Is it kind?* When leaders pass their messages through that filter, they conserve power. Their language gains weight because it carries no waste.

Leaders who remain above the line demonstrate that respect and realism are not opposites. They tell hard truths gently and gentle truths firmly. They create climates where facts can coexist with empathy. That equilibrium transforms performance from pressure to purpose.

Leadership AF Lesson: The Higher Your Awareness, the Lower Your Ego

Awareness and ego cannot share the same altitude. The climb toward awareness demands releasing the ballast of self-importance. Each increase in perspective lightens identity's grip. Leaders who understand this find that authority deepens as ego dissolves. They stop performing leadership and start embodying it. Their decisions become quieter, their impact larger.

Awareness lowers ego not through self-denial but through proportion. It reminds leaders that they are part of something vast: a timeline, a community, a continuum of effort. From that vantage point, success feels like stewardship rather than conquest. Praise becomes gratitude. Criticism becomes data.

Every interaction becomes an opportunity to learn.

The truly aware leader stops competing with their team and begins collaborating with reality. They move beyond proving competence to cultivating competence in others. Ego seeks validation; awareness seeks connection. Ego isolates; awareness integrates. The cultural results are unmistakable: transparency increases, defensiveness decreases, and collective intelligence rises.

When an organization learns to think this way, mistakes no longer trigger panic. They trigger inquiry. Leaders ask, *What pattern produced this?* rather than *Who caused this?* Lessons compound; trust compounds faster. The workplace shifts from judgment to refinement.

Awareness also changes how power feels from the inside. Ego uses power to protect itself; awareness uses power to protect purpose. Ego hoards credit; awareness shares it. Ego fears dissent; awareness invites it. The leader who can welcome contradiction without losing composure multiplies innovation. Disagreement becomes a form of devotion to truth.

The long game of awareness is freedom—freedom from impulsive reaction, from emotional debt, from the tyranny of always needing to be right. It frees creative energy once wasted on defensiveness and redirects it toward building, mentoring, imagining. The most liberated leaders are those least governed by pride.

At its height, staying above the line becomes an ethical stance. It says that clarity is a form of kindness, that listening is an act of respect, and that composure under fire is a moral choice. These are not small matters in a world starved for integrity. Awareness is how leadership keeps its soul.

Leaders who live this way do not claim perfection; they claim consciousness. They still stumble, still feel anger and fear, but they know the way back. They practice the climb daily. Their example teaches that the standard is not never falling—it is never staying fallen. That lesson, repeated across a culture, becomes collective resilience.

As awareness spreads, even conflict changes texture. Arguments give way to dialogue, and dialogue gives way to discovery. People stop fighting for dominance and start searching for accuracy. The line between right and wrong blurs into a gradient of learning. The organization becomes less a battlefield and more a workshop for truth.

Such a culture is not utopian; it is disciplined. It requires leaders who will pause when impatience flares, breathe when tension spikes, and re-center when chaos calls. This is not weakness—it is craftsmanship of the mind. It is leadership forged in the quiet forge of reflection.

When awareness defines leadership, results follow naturally. Efficiency improves because energy is no longer lost to ego. Retention improves because respect replaces fear. Innovation improves because safety liberates creativity.

Awareness is not the opposite of performance; it is its foundation.

The world remembers loud leaders, but it relies on aware ones. Noise fades; clarity endures. Staying above the line does not make leaders larger than life—it makes them fully alive within it.

In the end, the line is not a rule to follow but a reminder to return. Every moment invites the same choice: to react or to reflect, to descend into ego or ascend into awareness. The difference seems small, yet history turns on it.

Leadership that stays above the line becomes more than management—it becomes mentorship, culture, and legacy all at once. Its influence is quiet, cumulative, and unstoppable.

Because staying above the line does not make a leader better than anyone—it makes them better for everyone.

The longer awareness is practiced, the more it becomes an ethical technology—a method for aligning inner order with outer impact. Modern neuroscience shows that when leaders pause before reacting, the prefrontal cortex—the part of the brain responsible for reasoning and empathy—stays online. When they don't, the amygdala floods the body with cortisol and adrenaline. Biology itself confirms the ancient wisdom: reflection widens choice; reactivity narrows it. The line is not moral in origin—it is neurological. It marks the boundary between primitive impulse and conscious intention.

Leaders who study this find that awareness conserves energy. Each emotional reaction avoided is energy reclaimed for problem-solving. A day filled with irritation may feel busy, but it produces nothing. A day guided by presence often feels slower while accomplishing more. The paradox of awareness is efficiency through stillness.

Cultures that live above the line share that rhythm. Their meetings include pauses, not as silence but as structure. Their debates are sharp yet safe. Their metrics include morale as seriously as money because they know that awareness multiplies profit indirectly—through retention, innovation, and trust. Awareness is measurable; it just doesn't fit neatly on a spreadsheet.

Below-the-line cultures, by contrast, run on noise. They confuse urgency with importance, reaction with responsiveness. Their leaders praise "speed" even as they exhaust judgment. In those environments, burnout is not an individual failure; it is a cultural reflex. The antidote is awareness elevated to policy—scheduled reflection, mindful communication, and emotional literacy built into evaluation.

Philosophically, the line represents the human struggle between gravity and lift. Gravity pulls toward certainty, control, and self-protection. Lift draws toward curiosity, humility, and shared purpose. Both are constant. Leadership is the practice of generating enough lift to counter gravity's pull without denying its existence. No one lives permanently in the sky. But every conscious ascent reminds people that flying is possible.

When organizations institutionalize awareness, decision-making changes texture. Metrics remain, but meaning expands. Teams begin asking not only "Did we succeed?" but "What did we learn?" Failure becomes information,

CHAPTER 12: STAY ABOVE THE LINE

not identity. The culture becomes adaptive rather than reactive. From that altitude, even conflict becomes collaboration.

Awareness also clarifies morality in ambiguous situations. The question "Is this right?" shifts from legal compliance to human consequence. Awareness notices who is absent from the table, who is unheard, who pays the unseen cost of a quick decision. Ethical clarity emerges from empathy guided by logic, not from rules enforced by fear.

History remembers revolutions led by awareness. Social progress, scientific discovery, artistic innovation—all begin when someone steps above the reflex of conformity and chooses to see freshly. That same courage, scaled to daily leadership, keeps organizations humane. Awareness is civil disobedience against automatic thinking.

There is also tenderness in this practice. Awareness makes leaders gentler, not softer. It reveals how fragile trust can be, how easily dignity can be bruised by a careless tone. That realization reshapes authority. Orders become invitations. Corrections become conversations. Control gives way to guidance. The shift seems subtle but it changes how people feel at work—and how they go home.

Sustained awareness even alters time's geometry. When attention deepens, moments stretch. In a crisis, an aware leader experiences clarity rather than blur. They register detail—the tremor in a voice, the implication in a sentence—because they are present enough to perceive it. This temporal expansion creates better decisions and a kind of quiet grace under pressure.

The greatest leaders treat awareness as craftsmanship. They polish it through solitude, reading, journaling, and honest feedback. They study themselves as carefully as their markets. They ask, *What patterns of thought keep repeating?* and *What emotion am I mistaking for truth?* This self-inquiry is not vanity; it is maintenance of integrity. Without it, even good intentions corrode into habit.

There are practical ways to anchor this philosophy. Some leaders begin meetings with a moment of centering—one breath before business. Others debrief not just outcomes but emotional climates: *How did this feel? What shifted today?* Small rituals build large awareness. They remind teams that thoughtfulness is not delay but discipline.

Awareness also reshapes ambition. It redirects drive from recognition to contribution. Ambition below the line asks, *How can I stand out?* Above it asks, *How can I serve better?* The first ends with exhaustion; the second renews itself through meaning. When a whole organization adopts that orientation, competition turns into collective excellence.

Every generation inherits a choice: continue reacting as our ancestors did or evolve awareness as our advantage. The context changes—technology, politics, culture—but the line remains constant. Civilization itself is the ongoing attempt to stay above it.

Over time, awareness becomes its own reward. It allows leaders to enjoy the present without possession. They appreciate effort without clinging to outcome. They discover that composure is not the absence of passion but the governance of it. Emotion becomes a loyal ally rather than an unpredictable master.

Eventually, the practice matures into presence that others can feel. People enter the leader's office agitated and leave calmer. They can't name why; they simply mirror steadiness. This is the unspoken transmission of awareness— the way integrity radiates beyond words. It is why certain people change rooms without speeches: they embody equilibrium.

As awareness expands, gratitude follows. Leaders begin to see that even conflict is evidence of care, that frustration signals investment. They stop resenting friction and start respecting it. Gratitude shifts the inner dialogue from *Why is this happening to me?* to *What is this giving me?* and that shift changes how leadership feels from burden to privilege.

Every long-term legacy shares one trait: continuity of awareness. Strategies outdate, technologies vanish, but cultures built on mindfulness sustain. They survive economic storms and generational turnover because their foundation is internal, not external. They are led by people who understand that emotional intelligence is the renewable energy of organizations.

Awareness also breeds courage of a quieter kind—the courage to remain kind when others are cruel, to remain patient when others demand haste, to remain principled when expediency beckons. It is resistance without aggression. In such restraint lies the deepest strength.

There will always be moments of descent. The line is not a summit but a cycle. Fatigue, disappointment, and ego will drag every leader below it at times. What matters is agility—the speed of return. Awareness shortens recovery. Reflection becomes a ladder. Humility supplies the rungs.

And gradually, the philosophy that began as discipline becomes identity. Leaders no longer *try* to stay above the line; they simply notice when they are not. Awareness becomes self-correcting. Ego still whispers, but it no longer commands.

As organizations filled with such leaders spread, society itself edges upward. The microclimates of awareness—offices, classrooms, households—merge into weather patterns of compassion. Leadership, multiplied through consciousness, becomes civilization's immune system.

In the final analysis, staying above the line is not about serenity—it is about stewardship. It is choosing clarity over chaos for the sake of others. It is recognizing that leadership is less a privilege to be enjoyed than a responsibility to remain aware on behalf of those who cannot.

And now, as this reflection turns personal, one truth rises from all the philosophy: leadership is never abstract. It is a daily, human, fragile act. It happens in traffic, in hallways, in arguments and apologies. The line appears everywhere because awareness is always waiting for rehearsal.

So remember this: awareness is not a mountain to climb but a horizon to face. Each morning, leaders stand before it. Some rush ahead, blinded by urgency; others pause long enough to see the view. The ones who pause—who breathe, who notice, who choose calm over chaos—carry the world a little higher.

That is the quiet revolution of staying above the line. It doesn't roar; it steadies. It doesn't boast; it builds. And it begins, always, with one conscious breath—one leader deciding that presence itself is leadership.

Lead that way. Stay above the line. And watch everything you influence begin to rise with you.

Chapter 13: The Power of Humility

"Humility isn't thinking less of yourself; it's thinking of yourself less."

Humility is leadership's quiet superpower. It doesn't shout, it doesn't demand attention, and it never tries to be impressive. But it changes everything it touches. Where pride divides, humility connects. Where ego blinds, humility sees clearly. Every strong culture, every lasting legacy, and every great leader has one thing in common—they learned how to lead without making it about themselves.

The world often confuses humility with weakness, but that's a lie. True humility isn't self-doubt—it's self-awareness. It's knowing exactly who you are, what you're capable of, and where you still need to grow. It's confidence without arrogance and strength without showmanship. Humility doesn't shrink; it steadies.

Pride screams, "Look at me." Humility whispers, "How can I help?" And that whisper moves mountains. The leader who puts people before ego earns a kind of authority that can't be taken away. Titles can be revoked; respect can't. Humility earns what power demands.

Leadership AF Lesson:
Ego seeks credit; humility seeks progress.

Humility doesn't mean letting people walk over you. It means walking beside them. It's the ability to correct without condescension, to guide without superiority, and to serve without keeping score. Humble leaders don't need

CHAPTER 13: THE POWER OF HUMILITY

to remind people of their authority—they show it through consistency and care. Their credibility speaks louder than their position.

When a humble leader walks onto a jobsite, people feel it. The tension drops. The communication flows. People start doing things not out of fear, but out of pride. That's because humility creates safety. It gives others permission to be human—to ask questions, admit mistakes, and keep learning. When people feel safe enough to be honest, excellence grows naturally.

Pride is loud but fragile. It needs validation to survive. Humility is quiet but unbreakable. It doesn't depend on applause because it's rooted in purpose. Pride collapses under pressure; humility stands taller the harder things get.

Leadership is full of moments where your ego will try to take the wheel—when someone questions your decision, when you feel overlooked, when a younger leader challenges your way of thinking. The humble leader pauses, listens, and learns. The proud one reacts, defends, and resists. One grows stronger; the other grows smaller.

Humility transforms correction into connection. When you correct someone from pride, it sounds like blame. When you correct them from humility, it sounds like belief. "I expect more from you because I believe in you" lands differently than "You need to do better." Same goal, different spirit. The difference is humility.

Humility also changes how we handle success. Pride wants the spotlight. Humility shares it. When something goes right, the humble leader gives credit to the team. They don't hoard praise; they distribute it. That generosity builds trust. Because when people know their leader won't take the glory for their effort, they'll give even more effort.

One of the best measures of humility is how a leader handles being wrong. Everyone makes mistakes—but not everyone admits them. Pride hides. Humility owns it. "That one's on me" might be five of the most powerful words in leadership. It tells your team you value truth more than image. It makes you relatable, not unreachable. And relatability is the gateway to influence.

People will forgive your mistakes faster than they'll forgive your pride. Pride isolates; humility invites. The leader who can say, "I don't know," opens the door for collaboration. They turn uncertainty into opportunity. They make room for ideas bigger than their own.

I once worked with a project manager who seemed unshakable. When something went wrong, he didn't assign blame. He asked questions. He didn't boast when things went right. He thanked his team. His calm wasn't weakness—it was mastery. He didn't need to prove he was in charge; his presence made it obvious. That's the power of humility—it doesn't announce authority; it embodies it.

Humility also changes how we handle feedback. Pride hears feedback as insult; humility hears it as instruction. Leaders who can receive feedback with curiosity instead of defensiveness grow faster than anyone else. They don't waste energy protecting their image—they invest energy improving their impact.

The higher you climb in leadership, the harder humility becomes. Success whispers lies. It tells you you've figured it all out, that your way is the best way, that you've earned the right to stop listening. That's the moment humility matters most—when you think you don't need it.

Humility keeps leaders teachable. It keeps their perspective fresh. It keeps their influence clean. Because the moment you believe you're above learning, you've already started falling. Pride falls fast because it blinds its host to the slope beneath them. Humility keeps your feet on the ground, no matter how high you rise.

Humility also has a quiet way of defusing conflict. It listens first, talks second, and apologizes quickly. It doesn't take offense where none was meant, and it doesn't waste energy proving points. The humble leader's focus isn't on being right—it's on making things right. That's the difference between ego and influence.

When you lead with humility, people follow because they *want* to, not because they *have* to. They trust your motives. They know you'll tell them the truth, even when it's uncomfortable, and you'll take responsibility when things go sideways. That kind of credibility is rare—and it's magnetic.

Humility and accountability walk hand in hand. A humble leader doesn't make excuses. They don't shift blame. They own their role in every outcome.

CHAPTER 13: THE POWER OF HUMILITY

They don't have to defend their integrity because they live it daily. When your team sees that, they start mirroring it. Ownership becomes contagious.

The humble leader doesn't chase recognition; they chase results. They're not in competition with others—they're in collaboration with them. They measure success not by how many people they command, but by how many they lift.

Humility is not about downplaying yourself; it's about elevating others. It's the courage to let someone else shine without feeling smaller in the process. A proud leader competes with their team; a humble one completes it. They understand that success is a shared story, not a solo act.

Humility also protects you from the burnout that comes with trying to be everything to everyone. When you believe you have to carry all the answers, fix all the problems, and control all the outcomes, pride slowly becomes a burden. Humility lets you breathe. It reminds you that leadership is about guidance, not perfection. It gives you permission to say, "I need help," without shame.

That kind of honesty is liberating. It builds connection because people can finally see the real you — not the polished mask of authority, but the human being behind it. And people will follow authenticity far longer than they'll follow authority.

The power of humility also shows up in how you respond to success. A humble leader celebrates victories but never lets them rewrite reality. They don't start believing they're invincible; they remember the lessons that got them there. Every win becomes a reminder of teamwork, timing, and grace — not a monument to self.

Pride makes leaders believe they've arrived. Humility reminds them they're still becoming. That mindset keeps you hungry, curious, and open. It keeps you teachable. And teachability is the ultimate form of strength because it means you can adapt faster than prideful people who refuse to grow.

Humility is also contagious. When you model it, others mirror it. Conversations become more honest. Conflicts shrink faster. People stop jockeying for credit and start fighting for solutions. Suddenly, the culture shifts — less competition, more collaboration. Less noise, more trust.

A humble culture doesn't mean everyone's soft; it means everyone's strong enough to set ego aside for the mission. That's what humility does — it makes room for excellence. Because when people stop protecting their pride, they start protecting the purpose.

The irony of leadership is that the more humility you show, the more respect you earn. People want to work for leaders who can listen, admit when they're wrong, and give credit freely. They want to feel seen, not managed. Humility creates that environment because it decentralizes power.

It makes everyone feel like a stakeholder in success.

I've seen powerful transformations happen when leaders learned to say three simple phrases:

"I was wrong."

"I don't know."

"Thank you."

Those words disarm ego and build trust faster than any management strategy ever could. They're short, but they carry the full weight of authenticity.

Humility doesn't erase confidence — it refines it. A humble leader is confident enough to take risks, to fail publicly, and to grow openly. They don't hide behind excuses because their worth isn't tied to being right all the time. They've learned that credibility grows in the soil of honesty.

Leadership AF Lesson:
Humility doesn't weaken authority; it humanizes it.

Humility is also what keeps leadership from turning into domination. Without it, power becomes toxic. Pride creates leaders who believe they're the smartest in the room; humility creates leaders who build rooms full of smart people. Pride isolates; humility integrates. Pride inflates; humility elevates.

In tough times, humility is often mistaken for uncertainty. But in truth, it's the anchor that holds steady when arrogance would crack. Pride refuses help until it's too late. Humility asks for input early and prevents the fall. It

CHAPTER 13: THE POWER OF HUMILITY

doesn't panic — it pivots.

Humility also teaches patience — the discipline of not rushing people's growth or demanding instant results. A humble leader knows progress takes time. They give others space to learn, to make mistakes, to improve. That patience builds loyalty, and loyalty builds legacy.

And when a humble leader wins, they don't celebrate alone. They look around and see the hands that helped, the minds that solved, and the hearts that stayed committed. They know leadership is never a solo accomplishment — it's always a team symphony.

The longer you lead, the more you realize that humility isn't a leadership strategy — it's a survival skill. It keeps your vision clear, your relationships strong, and your ego in check. It allows you to keep learning, keep listening, and keep leading even after the applause fades.

Pride makes noise. Humility makes impact. The first demands recognition; the second earns it.

The power of humility lies in its paradox: the more you give it away, the more you gain. You gain peace. You gain clarity. You gain influence that doesn't need to be announced — it's just felt. People walk away from you not feeling smaller, but stronger. That's the quiet miracle of humble leadership: it multiplies strength by sharing it.

In the end, humility is the foundation of every trait we admire in great leaders — integrity, empathy, courage, and wisdom. Because without humility, those traits collapse under pride. But with humility, they endure pressure, success, and time.

So stay grounded. Stay teachable. Stay grateful.

Be the kind of leader who doesn't need the last word, the spotlight, or the title to make an impact.

Be the leader who lifts others higher.

Because in the long run, the loudest leaders fade — but the humble ones last forever.

Chapter 14: The Servant Leader

"A true leader doesn't stand above their people—they stand beneath them, holding them up."

The greatest misconception about leadership is that it's about power. It isn't. Real leadership is about service. It's about rolling up your sleeves, stepping into the mess, and making life better for the people you lead. Titles might grant authority, but only service earns loyalty.

Servant leadership isn't weakness—it's strength in its purest form. It's the strength to set your ego aside, to listen instead of lecture, to carry weight that others can't, and to put your people before yourself without losing your standards. It's the art of leading from the middle, not the top.

You can spot a servant leader immediately. They're the ones checking on their team before checking their emails. They're the ones who make time for people even when their schedule says they shouldn't. They're not chasing applause or validation—they're chasing impact. They're not trying to look good; they're trying to do good.

The servant leader doesn't measure success by how many people answer to them, but by how many people rise because of them. They know leadership isn't about being in charge—it's about taking care of those in your charge. That's not poetic language; it's operational truth. Because when people feel cared for, they perform better, communicate more openly, and protect the culture that protects them.

Service-centered leadership begins with one question: *What do my people need to succeed?* Sometimes the answer is tools. Sometimes it's time.

CHAPTER 14: THE SERVANT LEADER

Sometimes it's encouragement. Sometimes it's a hard conversation. Servant leaders don't give people what's easiest—they give them what's needed.

The job of leadership isn't to build followers; it's to build other leaders. Service is how you do that. You empower, support, and equip your people until they no longer need your supervision. That's success—not dependency, but development. When your team starts solving problems without waiting for permission, you've shifted from control to capability.

Servant leadership doesn't mean saying yes to everything. It means saying yes to what matters. It means protecting your people from unnecessary chaos and guiding them through the storms that can't be avoided. It's not about pleasing everyone—it's about prioritizing the mission and the people equally.

When a servant leader walks onto a site, people feel safer—not just physically, but emotionally. They know this is someone who will listen, who will back them up, who will own their mistakes alongside them. That sense of security unlocks performance. People will go the extra mile for a leader who they know would walk it for them.

Servant leadership is patient but not passive. It acts decisively when needed but never from arrogance. It leads with empathy, but not indulgence. It's the rare balance between compassion and conviction—the ability to care deeply while still holding firm to expectations.

The best servant leaders lead through questions, not commands. "What do you think?" "How can we fix this?" "What do you need from me?" Those questions transfer ownership. They teach people to think instead of just follow. That's how leaders multiply themselves—by turning service into empowerment.

Many leaders think serving their people will make them look soft. The truth is the opposite. Servant leaders earn more respect because their strength is proven, not performed. Anyone can demand effort; few can inspire it. The difference lies in intention. When people know your motives are pure, they'll give you everything they've got.

Service also changes how a leader handles accountability. When a servant leader enforces a rule or issues a correction, it doesn't come from ego—it comes from love. "I'm not correcting you because you failed me; I'm correcting you because you deserve better than this." That message lands differently. It builds trust instead of resentment.

Leadership AF Lesson:
You can't lead people effectively until you learn to serve them sincerely.

Servant leadership is built on humility. It means you're not too proud to sweep the floor, carry materials, or help solve problems that others think are beneath them. That doesn't mean you do everything yourself—it means you do whatever it takes. You model effort so that effort becomes culture.

When your people see you take responsibility for things you could have delegated, it sends a message: "No task is beneath me." That message echoes. Soon enough, they'll start carrying that same mindset into their own work. Because leadership, when done right, doesn't just lead people—it teaches them how to lead.

Being a servant leader also means seeing the individual within the role. People aren't job titles or production units—they're human beings with strengths, struggles, and stories. When you take time to understand what drives them, what challenges them, and what they're proud of, you unlock potential that no motivational speech ever could.

There's a quiet power in asking, "How are you doing, really?" and meaning it. Because when your people realize you see them beyond their output, they'll give you loyalty beyond their paycheck. That's what servant leadership builds—loyalty that's not bought, but earned.

Servant leadership requires constant self-awareness. It's easy to start serving from ego—doing things for recognition instead of genuine care. True service expects nothing in return. It's the quiet kind of help that doesn't need to be announced. It's the leadership that works while others watch.

This doesn't mean you let people walk over you or ignore standards. Servant leaders aren't pushovers—they're protectors. They protect people *and* performance. They understand that care without accountability breeds chaos, and accountability without care breeds resentment. Balance both, and you build something extraordinary: trust.

CHAPTER 14: THE SERVANT LEADER

When trust grows, control becomes unnecessary. Your team starts leading themselves. They start taking initiative. They start owning the culture. And that's the moment every servant leader lives for—the moment they realize they've built something that can thrive without them.

Servant leadership isn't about sacrifice without boundaries. It's about stewardship. You're not giving everything away — you're giving what you have so others can stand taller. A servant leader knows that leadership is borrowed power, not permanent possession. It's loaned to you for the sake of the mission and the people, and you prove worthy of it by using it for their good.

The heart of service is presence. People don't need a leader who only shows up for the big speeches or the easy days. They need one who's there in the grind — in the rain, the confusion, the cleanup. That's where credibility grows. People don't remember what you said when things were calm; they remember how you acted when things were hard.

Service makes you resilient. When you lead for yourself, every failure feels personal. But when you lead for others, failure becomes fuel. You learn faster because you're learning for the sake of something bigger than your ego. And that kind of purpose can outlast any setback.

Servant leadership also prevents burnout — not by working less, but by working with meaning. When your energy comes from helping people grow, you stop measuring hours and start measuring impact. Service fills what stress drains. It keeps your fire lit even when the winds of adversity blow hard.

Great servant leaders understand that their real work is invisible. The best parts of what they do will never make it into reports or newsletters. It happens in the quiet moments — the private check-ins, the calm after the storm, the encouraging word that changes someone's entire day. That's where leadership lives: in the unseen spaces where people are built.

When you lead with service, you start to see the ripple effect. You help one person, and they help another. You steady one team, and the next project runs smoother. Over time, those ripples become waves that change the entire culture. That's the power of service: it scales without shouting.

The servant leader doesn't wait for recognition, but recognition always finds them. Because results speak louder than ego. Teams led by servants outperform those led by tyrants — not because they work harder, but because they work with heart. You can't fake that. When people believe in their leader, they believe in their work.

Service is also the cure for arrogance. When you spend enough time helping others succeed, you stop obsessing over your own image. You start realizing that leadership is a cycle of giving and growing. You give knowledge, time, and attention — and in return, you grow patience, perspective, and gratitude.

That's the real return on investment.

A servant leader listens more than they speak. They don't just hear the words — they listen for what's behind them. They hear fear, frustration, hope, and ambition. They don't rush to respond; they absorb. That kind of listening doesn't just solve problems — it prevents them. Because most conflicts die quietly when people feel heard.

Servant leadership also sharpens fairness. When your motive is service, bias fades. You stop favoring the loudest voice or the easiest path. You make decisions based on what's right, not what's convenient. People sense that kind of integrity, and it anchors their trust.

Being a servant leader doesn't mean being perfect. It means being willing — willing to help, to grow, to take responsibility, and to admit when you don't know. It's a posture of learning, not lecturing. The best servant leaders are students of people. They study what motivates them, what frustrates them, what inspires them — and then they use that knowledge to lift them higher.

That's why servant leadership lasts longer than authority ever will. Authority fades when the title changes. Service leaves a legacy that lives in every person you touched along the way. Those people carry your lessons forward in their own leadership. That's multiplication at its finest.

The servant leader also understands timing. They know when to lead from the front, when to step aside, and when to push others forward. They understand that sometimes the best way to lead is to let someone else take the spotlight. Because if you've done your job right, your team doesn't need you to hold their hand — they need you to believe in their hands.

CHAPTER 14: THE SERVANT LEADER

True service changes how power feels. It no longer feels like control; it feels like responsibility. You stop using authority to get results and start using influence to grow people. That's how servant leaders turn command into connection.

There's an old saying: *If service is beneath you, leadership is beyond you.* That's the truth. If you can't kneel to help someone, you don't deserve the right to stand above them. Leadership isn't earned through speeches; it's earned through sweat and sincerity.

Servant leadership isn't glamorous, but it's glorious. It's the kind of leadership that doesn't need a plaque or a post. It lives on in the people who became better because you were there. They'll remember the way you made them feel — capable, trusted, valued — and that memory will keep your legacy alive long after your name fades from the org chart.

Leadership AF Lesson:
The measure of a leader is found in the strength of the people they leave behind.

Servant leadership is how cultures heal. It's how teams rebuild after burnout, how trust returns after mistakes, and how excellence sustains after success. Because service never stops—it keeps giving back long after the applause ends.

So, serve first. Lead second. Protect your people. Lift them up. Give them the credit and take the blame when you must. That's not weakness—that's warrior leadership. The kind that doesn't just build projects; it builds people.

In the end, your real legacy won't be in the policies you wrote or the profits you produced—it'll be in the people who now lead because of you.

Chapter 15: The Leader's Legacy

"You won't be remembered for how high you climbed, but for how many you lifted while you were climbing."

Legacy isn't something you leave behind when you're gone. It's something you build every day you show up. It's written in your actions, in the tone you set, and in the people you shape. The leader's legacy isn't carved in stone—it's carried in hearts. It's not about statues or slogans; it's about stories told quietly when your name comes up years later. Legacy has nothing to do with position and everything to do with presence. You don't need a title to build one. You build it through consistency, integrity, and the small moments that accumulate over time—the moments when you chose patience instead of pride, truth instead of comfort, service instead of spotlight.

Every choice you make as a leader leaves a mark. The way you handle conflict, the way you react under pressure, the way you treat people when nobody's watching—those are the brushstrokes of your legacy. You're painting every day, whether you realize it or not.

Leadership AF Lesson:
Your real legacy isn't what you leave for people—it's what you leave in them.

The problem is, most leaders think legacy is built at the end of their career. They imagine it as a moment—retirement speeches, plaques, or awards. But legacy isn't a final chapter; it's every sentence you've written along the way.

CHAPTER 15: THE LEADER'S LEGACY

It's in the culture you've shaped and the confidence you've inspired.

Some leaders chase numbers—sales, profits, production goals—and that's fine. But numbers fade. Someone will beat them next quarter. What doesn't fade is impact. Impact is measured in people who learned to lead because you believed in them. It's in the way they handle pressure the way you once did, the way they lift others the way you lifted them. That's legacy.

Legacy lives in the way people talk about you when you're not in the room. It's in the sentence that starts with, "You know, I learned this from..." Those are the echoes that outlast every accomplishment. The people who carry your lessons forward are your living proof that leadership mattered.

Legacy also shows up in the small, quiet decisions—the ones nobody applauds but everyone feels. When you choose to do the right thing instead of the easy one. When you treat someone with dignity even after they've disappointed you. When you admit a mistake in front of your team. Those moments ripple far beyond that day. They teach others what integrity looks like in motion.

It's easy to confuse visibility with legacy. Visibility is popularity; legacy is permanence. Popularity fades when trends shift. Legacy grows because truth doesn't go out of style. The world forgets titles, but it remembers character.

The leader's legacy isn't built on how much power they held—it's built on how much power they gave away. When you create leaders who lead with confidence and compassion, your influence becomes exponential. You're no longer just one person making a difference—you're a generation of impact in motion.

Every leader will leave a legacy; not every legacy will be good. Some leave fear behind. Some leave resentment. Some leave confusion. But the best leave clarity, belief, and example. They leave systems that make sense, standards that endure, and stories that inspire.

The legacy you build comes down to one question: *How did people feel after being led by you?* Did they feel smaller or stronger? Used or valued? Afraid or empowered? Those feelings are the fingerprints you leave on others. You can't fake them; they're felt.

When your people think of you years later, will they remember your demands or your development? Your criticism or your compassion? Your ego or your example? The answer to that question is your legacy in one word.

One of the most important truths about legacy is that it begins long before you realize it. You're already building it right now—in this moment, in this decision, in the next conversation you have. Every day is a deposit in the bank of remembrance.

Legacy also lives in what you tolerate. The standard you accept becomes the story others tell about your leadership. If you let carelessness slide, your name will one day be attached to carelessness. If you demand excellence with fairness, your name will stand for excellence. What you allow becomes who you are in the memory of others.

Leaders sometimes forget that people rarely remember what you said, but they always remember how you made them feel. The tone of your leadership becomes the texture of your legacy. Kindness doesn't make you weak—it makes you unforgettable.

Legacy isn't about being perfect; it's about being principled. People won't recall every decision you made, but they'll remember the spirit you led with. They'll remember the humility you showed when you were wrong, the courage you displayed when things were hard, and the grace you offered when others fell short.

When you focus on legacy, leadership becomes simpler. You stop leading for applause and start leading for impact. You stop chasing moments of glory and start creating moments of growth. You begin to see people not as resources, but as reflections of your values.

Legacy isn't something you declare; it's something others define for you. You don't get to decide what your legacy is—your actions already have. The way you show up each day is your legacy in progress. The leader's legacy isn't about what you build with your hands; it's about what you build in hearts and minds.

If you want to know what kind of legacy you're creating, look at the people around you. Are they growing? Do they trust each other? Are they proud of their work? Those are reflections of your leadership. A healthy culture is a leader's living résumé.

CHAPTER 15: THE LEADER'S LEGACY

Your words might inspire for a moment, but your consistency inspires for a lifetime. People will forget your speeches, but they won't forget the standard you lived by. They'll remember how you showed up when it mattered most.

Leadership is temporary, but legacy is transferable. It doesn't stop when you retire, resign, or move on. It lives on in the people who picked up your habits, your mindset, and your example. Every leader is a bridge to the next one. Your job isn't to be the destination—it's to make the path clear for those who'll walk after you.

A true leader measures success by succession. The question isn't "How well did I do?" but "How well will they do after me?" If the standard crumbles the moment you leave, then you built followers, not leaders. But if it holds—and even grows—then you built a legacy that breathes.

Leadership AF Lesson:
Your leadership ends when you stop showing up. Your legacy begins when they keep going without you.

Mentorship is where legacy multiplies. Every time you invest in someone's potential, you're extending your leadership beyond your lifetime. You become a living echo, shaping lives you'll never meet. That's the quiet immortality of influence.

You can't build legacy by talking about it—you build it by teaching it. You teach by showing what accountability looks like in action, what grace sounds like in conflict, what courage feels like under pressure. People don't learn leadership from memos; they learn it from proximity.

A leader's legacy isn't just measured in success—it's measured in survival. When your influence helps others endure, adapt, and keep moving long after you're gone, that's proof you led well. Legacy isn't about being remembered by everyone; it's about being remembered by the right ones—the ones you truly impacted.

The leader's legacy also depends on character. Charisma can open doors, but character keeps them open. It's what people say about you when they no longer need you. It's the difference between admiration and appreciation.

People may admire your results, but they'll appreciate your integrity.

Your reputation is what people think of you now. Your legacy is what they say when you're gone. Reputations fade fast, but legacies deepen over time. They grow stronger in the stories people tell about how you led, how you listened, how you lived.

Every decision you make is a seed. Some sprout fast; others take years to grow. Legacy leadership means planting trees whose shade you may never sit under. It means doing the right thing not because it benefits you now, but because it'll bless someone later.

The best legacies are built by leaders who were consistent in the little things. Showing up on time. Saying thank you. Keeping promises. Treating the janitor with the same respect as the CEO. Those aren't small acts—they're the daily bricks that build the foundation of trust your legacy rests on.

Legacy also comes from reflection. The strongest leaders take time to look back—not to relive the past, but to learn from it. They ask, "Did I leave things better than I found them?" That's the simplest and truest test of leadership.

Leaving things better doesn't mean perfection; it means progress. Did your team grow stronger? Did you help people find purpose? Did your culture become kinder, safer, more honest? If the answer is yes, then your legacy is secure.

The leader's legacy isn't built in grand gestures—it's built in consistency, compassion, and courage. The courage to tell the truth. The compassion to care even when it costs you. The consistency to show up even when no one's watching.

Leadership ends when your title changes. Legacy begins when your impact remains. And that impact doesn't have to be world-changing—it just has to be real. You don't have to build empires; you just have to build people who believe again.

Because the truth is, no one remembers every decision you made or every policy you wrote. But they'll always remember the leader who believed in them when they doubted themselves. They'll remember the one who saw more in them than they saw in themselves. That's the leader whose legacy outlives them.

CHAPTER 15: THE LEADER'S LEGACY

The leader's legacy is love translated into action, accountability expressed through service, and humility practiced under pressure. It's the daily discipline of choosing others over ego, purpose over pride, and meaning over medals.

Legacy isn't the echo of your name—it's the evidence of your character.

When your people lead others with the same compassion, conviction, and courage you once showed them, that's immortality. That's the proof your time here mattered.

And one day, when someone says your name in passing—quietly, with a hint of respect and a memory of gratitude—you'll know your legacy worked.

Because real leadership doesn't die. It just keeps leading through others.

That's your legacy.

That's the finish line.

That's how you lead like you've got a pair.

Closing Quote

"adership isn't about titles or power—it's about the lives you lift, the standards you raise, and the culture you leave behind." L
— C.E. Grayson Jr.
e

Thank You for Reading

Thank you for caring enough to grow as a leader. Every person who chooses to lead with integrity, courage, and respect strengthens the culture we all depend on.

Connect: www.linkedin.com/in/charlesgrayson80 Follow: AF Leadership Series updates and future releases.

Lead strong. Change culture. Save lives.

— C.E. Grayson Jr.

Metadata & Publishing Info

Title: Lead Like You Got a Pair: Change Culture. Save Lives.
Author: C.E. Grayson Jr.
Series: AF Leadership Series (Book 3)
Trim Size: 6 x 9 inches
Publisher: Kindle Direct Publishing
ISBN: 9798273528239
Language: English
Copyright: © 2025 C.E. Grayson Jr.
Keywords: Leadership, Safety, Accountability, Culture Change, Integrity, Management

AF Leadership Series Catalog

Book 1 – AF Mindset: Own It. Live It. Lead It.

The all-in mindset that builds confidence, integrity, and unstoppable drive.

Book 2 – You're Boring AF, Gary!

Bringing life, humor, and energy back into leadership—making safety engaging again.

Book 3 – Lead Like You Got a Pair: Change Culture. Save Lives.

The blueprint for courageous leadership that transforms attitude into action.

Book 4 – Safe AF: A Sidekick for the Everyday Safety Professional

A pocket-size companion for real-world safety leadership and confidence on the job.

Made in the USA
Coppell, TX
14 November 2025

63092756R10079